HOW TO
SURVIVE
MERCURY
RETROGRADE

© Keith Papke

About the Author

Bernie Ashman has been a professional astrologer for over thirty years, having discovered his passion for astrology while reading Dane Rudhyar's *Astrology of Personality*. Since that time, his astrology practice has expanded to include writing, lecturing, and counseling clients from all over the world. He is now a recognized authority in the astrology field, and his writings have earned accolades from his readers and peers alike.

"I see astrology as a wonderful blueprint in assisting individuals to more clearly define their life choices," says Ashman, and his person-centered approach to astrology has made him a favorite with his readers. Ashman is known for his ability to make even the most complex topics accessible to the novice astrologer.

Ashman is the author of *SignMates: Understanding the Games People Play* (Llewellyn, 2000), *Intuition and Your Sun Sign* (Llewellyn, 2014), *Sun Signs & Past Lives* (Llewellyn, 2010), *Astrological Games People Play* (ACS, 1987), and *Roadmap to Your Future* (ACS, 1994; reprinted by the American Federation of Astrologers, 2000). He has also written articles that are posted on the Llewellyn website, and his articles have appeared in several magazines and journals, including *Dell Horoscope*, *Astro Signs*, *The Mountain Astrologer*, and *Welcome to Planet Earth*. His insightful interpretations have also been used for astrology software programs used worldwide, most recently by Cosmic Patterns.

HOW TO SURVIVE MERCURY RETROGRADE

[AND VENUS & MARS, TOO]

BERNIE ASHMAN

Llewellyn Publications
Woodbury, Minnesota

FIRST EDITION
First Printing, 2016

Cover design: Ellen Lawson
Cover images: iStockphoto.com/14407038/©parameter
               iStockphoto.com/27892612/©MarcelC

Llewellyn Publications is a registered trademark of Llewellyn Worldwide Ltd.

Library of Congress Cataloging-in-Publication Data
Names: Ashman, Bernie.
Title: How to survive Mercury retrograde : and Venus & Mars, too / by Bernie Ashman.
Description: FIRST EDITION. | Woodbury : Llewellyn Worldwide. Ltd., 2016.
Identifiers: LCCN 2015039071 (print) | LCCN 2015041772 (ebook) | ISBN 9780738745176 | ISBN 9780738747415 ()
Subjects: LCSH: Astrology. | Mercury (Planet)—Miscellanea. | Venus (Planet)—Miscellanea. | Mars (Planet)—Miscellanea.
Classification: LCC BF1724 .A84 2016 (print) | LCC BF1724 (ebook) | DDC 133.5/3—dc23
LC record available at http://lccn.loc.gov/2015039071

Llewellyn Worldwide Ltd. does not participate in, endorse, or have any authority or responsibility concerning private business transactions between our authors and the public.

All mail addressed to the author is forwarded, but the publisher cannot, unless specifically instructed by the author, give out an address or phone number.

Any Internet references contained in this work are current at publication time, but the publisher cannot guarantee that a specific location will continue to be maintained. Please refer to the publisher's website for links to authors' websites and other sources.

Llewellyn Publications
A Division of Llewellyn Worldwide Ltd.
2143 Wooddale Drive
Woodbury, MN 55125-2989
www.llewellyn.com

Printed in the United States of America

Other Books by Bernie Ashman

Intuition and Your Sun Sign
(Llewellyn Publications, 2014)

Sun Signs & Past Lives: Your Soul's Evolutionary Path
(Llewellyn Publications, 2010)

SignMates: Understanding the Games People Play
(Llewellyn Publications, 2000)

Astrological Games People Play
(ACS Publications, 1987)

Roadmap to Your Future
(ACS Publications, 1994; reprinted by the AFA, 2000)

Contents

Introduction

Welcome to a book that is a primer on how to survive retrograde planets. The purpose of this book is to help you be better prepared for a retrograde cycle and learn not to fear a planet when it is retrograde. You will read in the following pages how to arm yourself with the knowledge to handle those areas of life that will most likely be affected by a retrograde planet. You will be shown how to avoid negative tendencies or thoughts during a retrograde period and, very importantly, how to take advantage of the opportunities offered by retrograde planets. This book will help you make better informed decisions about relationships, communication issues, and business matters during a retrograde cycle. There is no beginner book on retrograde planets available today quite like this one. Whether you are a student of astrology, an astrologer, or just someone wanting to know how to survive a retrograde cycle with less stress, you have definitely come to the right book.

A retrograde cycle refers to the duration of time a planet remains retrograde, or moving backward, through an astrological sign before once again moving in direct motion. It is important to know when there is a change of direction by a planet from direct to retrograde or retrograde to direct. Why? Because in timing your actions, it helps to know exactly when these changes of direction occur. This book will show you how to identify those time periods and the best way to handle them.

Retrograde planets are magical, in my opinion, because sometimes they will surprise you with new ideas and insights. A retrograde planet should not be underestimated in its potential to deliver the results you require to accomplish your hopes and dreams. As you will see, these retrograde cycles can take you to the land of success. A planet when in its retrograde cycle can inspire you to trust your intuition and ideas in the same way as when the planet is moving direct in motion. Through reading this book, you can tap into a new sense of empowerment. For those of you already familiar with retrograde planets, you might find a new way of thinking about this area of astrology.

A major focus of this book is how to survive retrograde time periods by offering you *survival tips*. These important tips will allow you to be more mentally sharp and assured that you can preserve your creative power and enjoy your life. You can pick and choose the survival tips that will work best for you during a retrograde time period. Each planetary retrograde is unique in its own way. The decisions you need to make during one retrograde could be completely different during another one. This book covers survival tips for retrogrades from several different angles to give you plenty of material to handle the challenges you might encounter. So rest assured that you will be well prepared to live your life confidently and comfortably.

Astrologers refer to the current movement of a planet through an astrological sign as a *transit*. The three faster-moving planets, which are the ones discussed in this book, are Mercury, Venus, and Mars. These three planets impact our everyday life experiences. You are not alone in trying to figure out the best way to make use of them. These planets are key motivators in opening our eyes to new opportunities. To give you a quick preview as to how they work, Mercury stimulates your communication, Venus inspires your quest to create harmony in your relationships, and Mars pushes you to act with decisiveness. You will see that each has a unique purpose, whether the planet is moving direct or retrograde. When moving retrograde, these planets challenge us to act with greater wisdom but not necessarily to back away from pursuing new goals—quite the contrary. You will see that a retrograde cycle can launch you forward with just as much clarity as when the planet is moving direct.

This book will also help you better perceive when people you know are undergoing some of the same challenges. When you realize you are not alone in dealing with a retrograde planet's challenges, this may point the way to tuning in to what someone else is thinking and feeling, creating a mutual understanding.

Chapter 5 provides answers to the most commonly asked questions about retrograde planets, such as should you sign a contract while Mercury is in retrograde motion? Is it okay to make a career change during a retrograde cycle?

Enjoy your journey through the chapters that follow. They are intended to make your life easier during a retrograde time period. You don't need to let your worries get the best of you during a retrograde cycle. The many survival tips provided in each planet chapter will help you find and enjoy a clear sense of purpose. Let this book encourage you to see the positive directions in which a retrograde planet can take you!

Chapter One

Retrograde Planets and What They Can Offer You

What Is a Retrograde Planet?

Retrograde simply describes the apparent backward motion of a planet through the zodiac or an astrological sign when the planet is observed from the earth. Essentially, a faster-moving planet is passing a slower-moving planet, creating the illusion that the slower planet is moving backward, or retrograde. When you pass a car while driving, the car you are passing looks like it is moving backward. When you observe a faster-moving train passing a slower train, the slower one appears to be moving backward, but of course this is not true. They are both moving forward, but the slower train just looks like it is moving backward.

Except for the Sun and Moon, the remaining planets move in retrograde motion at various times during the year. Each planet has its own unique length of time in which it remains retrograde before resuming direct motion. This will be explained further in the Mercury, Venus, and Mars chapters that follow.

You are accustomed to looking at a clock moving in a clockwise, or forward, direction. Would it not seem peculiar if the clock suddenly started moving backward? You would wonder if you had entered a new or alternative dimension of reality. A planet moving retrograde is like a clock moving backward. This retrograde motion asks your mind to adjust to the messages it is sending from this temporary change in orbit. It's like it puts your mind in a different internal time zone. But don't worry. As you enter the first few days of a planet's retrograde motion, your mind usually will catch on to the beat and rhythm of the retrograde planet. It is this backward motion of a planet that will work with your thoughts in unique ways.

Retrograde Planets and Their Positive Influences

There are different opinions about the value of retrograde planets. Some people view retrogrades negatively, as though a retrograde planet can never lead to positive outcomes. These people will tell you to stop pretty much everything you are doing until the planet goes direct. This is not exactly realistic advice. Most of us can't just put our life on hold. There is too much that needs to get done. This idea that you must not put an idea into motion during a retrograde is really not true at all. You can still proceed with great results, without missing a beat.

It is a big mistake to doubt the creative possibilities you can discover during retrograde time periods. Insightful ideas can flourish at this time. A renewed determination to accomplish your goals can manifest. Clarifying what you need from others may become more important. It is true that a little more digging out of the details could be needed. A greater analysis of a situation to ensure its success might be called for to get a plan accomplished the way you want it done.

Another key theme about retrograde planets is that they offer you a chance to get a deeper glimpse into situations. You can put whatever you like under a microscope and see even more of the intricate details that might be hidden, the fine print that perhaps you've overlooked. This could be in the area of rethinking a goal or deciding what you need to purchase. You may be trying to decide if the price is really worth the time and money it will take to make the final payment on what you will owe. Getting your strategy to make a deal go in your favor sometimes crystallizes under the movement of a retrograde. You may decide to reevaluate your decision to sign an important contract that involves a major commitment of your time and resources.

Rehashing what you want to communicate to others can become clearer during a retrograde. A deeper analysis of a better way to approach someone once again to work out your differences can become lucid. Retrograde energy has a unique way of pointing you toward a resolution to a question that you had not considered before.

Look at it this way. A retrograde planet can open your eyes to new options. It might be that you need to solve a problem. In many ways the research-oriented influence of these special cycles helps you probe beneath the surface of things to see the answer to an obstacle in your path. You may realize there is nothing to fix. Walking away might be in your best interest. Then again, you could muster up the courage to face the music, as the old saying goes, and deal directly with an issue. The bottom line here is that you will perceive an innovative direction in which to move.

Negative thinking can be turned around during a retrograde cycle. The redirecting of your energy can be accomplished. A lack of confidence can evolve into a greater belief in your ability. Think of a retrograde as an opportunity to rework your mental fortitude. The backward motion of a planet is a second chance at success. It might be the reprieve you need. This could provide you with a feeling that a great burden has been removed. This is no little thing in that it paves the way for you to put your best energy elsewhere.

You could feel more deserving of rewarding yourself for the hard work you've done. Rather than always thinking that delayed gratification must be your reality, you begin to see that there is nothing wrong with being good to yourself in the present. "The time is now" is more in your thinking. Giving is wonderful but so is receiving. Balancing the two experiences is more in your grasp. Retrogrades may open this up within your mind.

You can even break new ground in the midst of a retrograde time period. This may run contrary to what you have already heard about retrograde planets. Try to put aside any bias against retrograde motion. These cycles can offer the building ground for new ideas. Inventive instincts can flourish. It is very possible to take this energy forcefully out into the world. Your creative power might multiply and lead you to abundant new paths. The going over of important details allows you to more forcefully release your energy toward a goal. Perhaps it is in being very prepared for the future that allows this to occur.

Your communication ability can deepen, which is more typical during a Mercury retrograde time period. Learning new skills could open doors for new job opportunities. You may have a greater ability to form new alliances with people to empower you during a Venus retrograde. It might be that you are able to mend old wounds with others. A Mars retrograde may point the way to becoming more assertive. These retrograde cycles offer you a chance to leave past negative impulses behind. Self-confidence can overcome self-doubt. A new you can surface that you are proud to show the world.

How to Prepare and Use a Retrograde Cycle

Astrologers like myself are knowledgeable of when planets are about to enter their retrograde cycles to get a sense of the best way to stay productive. I like to be aware of when these cycles will begin and end to stay on top of what the current time period has to offer the clients I serve and for myself as well. The idea for all of us is to learn to flow with retrogrades without becoming too anxious and assuming life will go negatively. This is one of my main reasons for writing this book: to dispel some of the myths about retrograde planets. Another important purpose for writing the book is to offer survival tips so you can make the best use of your creative energy. The more alternatives you perceive to deal with circumstances that arise during a retrograde time period, the better off you will be. It will be that much easier to find your way around what appear to be roadblocks. The less discouraged you are, the easier it will be to stay on top of your goals.

In preparation for a retrograde cycle, one important thing is to think positive. This might sound like an oversimplification, but in my many years of experience it is one of the best ways to survive any retrograde period. Your creative energy will multiply when you continue to believe in yourself. One thing I have noticed is that individuals who experience retrograde cycles as misery often let their negative thoughts control them. You will attract a more positive experience if you maintain a levelheaded outlook. Staying grounded and centered really helps.

The main thing about any retrograde time period is to see it as an opportunity to make empowering choices. Think of retrograde planets as the universe's way of working with you to show you when it is best to push for what you need and when it is wise to hit the pause button. There may be a few stops and starts or do-overs. Try to maintain the mindset that practice makes for better outcomes during these retrograde cycles. You don't need to aim for perfection. Be reasonable with yourself in terms of expectations and all will probably go well.

If you are starting a project before a retrograde cycle begins and will still be involved with it during the retrograde period, don't be too worried. You can always make changes during the retrograde time period, if needed, without hurting your work and the careful planning you did in advance of the retrograde. Tweaking is inevitable. Think of this as a process. When the planet moves direct again, you may choose to make other changes. Just make your best effort to establish a plan of action before the retrograde. Prepare your mind that some changes will possibly be needed. Keeping your thoughts flexible will help you ride the ups and downs of a retrograde planet. Your life won't feel as stressful.

Some people like to make sure they have a project finished before a retrograde cycle begins. There is nothing wrong with this thinking either. It isn't the end of the world if you must make changes in the midst of a retrograde if it turns out that way. It is always a great idea to have as many of the details worked out as possible before a planet turns retrograde. Even if you finish a job before a retrograde begins, remember there is the chance that you will need to make a change or two during the retrograde time period.

Change is inevitable. Retrogrades teach us to accept the fact that life is a series of times when we need to adjust to changing circumstances. In many ways, planets when moving in retrograde motion are trying to guide us to focus more on our overall game plan and not get too caught up in the details.

Synchronicity and Retrograde Planets

Another perk of retrograde planets is that you might experience an event that appears to be a *meaningful coincidence*, or what is known as *synchronicity*. The inventor of this term, Carl Jung, described synchronicity as the meaningful coincidence of an event that has no causal explanation. You may have had a thought the day earlier about seeing an old friend whom you had not seen in several years and suddenly you run into them while shopping or you receive an email from them. Perhaps you'd thought about applying for a job at a particular company and you just happen to meet someone doing the hiring for that position at a social event. Was this merely an accident or was it the universe's way of making things happen for you? You might have had a dream about a situation and the next day it manifested just as you experienced in your dream. Retrograde planets do trigger these types of experiences at times.

So you see there is no sense in being overly anxious about retrogrades. They can work in ways that you could not imagine possible. If you maintain a positive mindset, the universe may bring you something you were hoping would occur. It is as though the forces at work are arranging these circumstances to happen at just the right time and place.

The Benefits of Tapping Into the Intuitive Energy of a Retrograde Cycle

Our brains are wired to think of time in a linear fashion. To survive the demands of living in a modern culture with busy schedules, we are pushed into using our left brain. To function logically and with a sense of order, our left brain comes in handy. The left brain is our analytical mind, unlike the more intuitive right brain. In my opinion, it is a good idea to learn to make use of both brain hemispheres.

Why am I talking about intuition in a book about retrograde planets? I have noticed that a retrograde planetary cycle can make it easier to tune in to the right brain. In other words, a retrograde planet can stimulate our use of intuition. Sometimes we move so fast through the day that we may not think it would be valuable to use our intuition or perhaps we just forget to use it.

A retrograde planetary cycle can feel like we have hit the rewind button in our lives. The retrograde time period of a planet lets us go back to investigate or rethink situations once again. Our intuition might tell us to relax and point us toward a more flowing way to solve a problem. There is an intuitive gift during a retrograde time period that we can discover.

Dreams can become more meaningful during retrograde cycles. It is as though the conscious mind finds it easier to move out of the way and let the intuitive mind receive symbolic messages. We may learn to appreciate the gift of a retrograde planet helping us solve a problem through delivering information through a dream. There is magic in retrograde cycles that might not be readily apparent when we are awake. Retrograde energy can move in mysterious ways.

There is even healing energy in retrograde cycles. These time periods can replenish our mental and physical energy. Even while we are busy at work or fulfilling our daily responsibilities, a retrograde planet may be working behind the scenes, empowering us with new insights. Don't ever underestimate what a retrograde planet can do for you in terms of filling you with creative energy.

There will be times when your intuition will point you toward the survival tips that can best help you handle a situation you are faced with during a planet's retrograde movement. There is a wonderful benefit in making use of your intuition. Each of the planet chapters that are now waiting for you to feast your mind and eyes on will offer you survival tips that will help you ease stress and create a more abundant life.

Chapter Two
Mercury:
The Communication Planet

Areas Influenced by Mercury: Communication, organizing, perception, learning, health

Elements Associated with Mercury: Air and earth

Signs Ruled by Mercury: Gemini and Virgo

Mercury Retrograde Gifts: Reinvigorated mental energy and new insights

Duration of Mercury Retrograde Cycle: Three weeks

Before we look at Mercury in its retrograde cycle, let's look at the way this planet works when moving direct. Mercury is the communication planet. The exchange of ideas is one of its primary functions. We are able to translate what we are saying to each other thanks to the help of this planet. Mercury helps you to absorb new learning and to develop a growing awareness of the world around you. In mythology, Mercury is known as the messenger of the gods. This planet tries to keep you mentally curious. Adapting to new situations is greatly aided by this planet's influence. Mercury is the ruler in astrology of two signs: airy Gemini and earthy Virgo. It is Mercury's Gemini side of things that pushes you to travel on the mental and physical levels. The Virgo expression of Mercury encourages you to be efficient and well organized in your actions. Both dimensions of Mercury are keys to moving successfully to get your daily activities accomplished with a sense of purpose.

Staying aware of new trends is another possible way Mercury can work with you. It will alert you to move with changing conditions. Adapting to new situations is a breeze when you tune in to this very resourceful, thought-oriented giant of the sky. Think of Mercury acting as a type of weather vane, helping you to tune in quickly to changing circumstances.

Your business instincts can be well developed and very organized when you are flowing with Mercury. Sensing how to make a deal in the blink of an eye is part of the Mercurial package, as is starting a business venture and keeping it a success. Keeping abreast of current trends is a way to keep a career or business pumping with enthusiasm. Your knowhow in staying ahead of competitors is another function of this mentally adept energy. Knowing what is working and what is not in a business depends heavily on Mercury's influence. Your ability to expand your management skills can flourish under the watchful eye of this planet. The confidence to keep operating at a high level in your place of work could help you get a promotion. Getting additional training and education gives you more options. Staying diversified in gaining knowledge helps you to have more than one way to earn a living. Mercury opens doors to work in multiple types of job functions at a time, improving your earning power.

A desire to share information is another key Mercurial theme. It activates the networker in you. The teacher and advisor part of your thought process comes alive when tuning in to this planet's symbolism. Wanting to excite others about learning might be in your thinking. Explaining concepts in easy-to-understand language is a possible talent. Breaking down what you are trying to communicate into small digestible parts can become a talent.

A desire to move in multiple directions simultaneously is another way to make use of Mercury. Juggling more than one responsibility in your life successfully with a keen awareness of remaining organized is yet another possible expression of Mercury. So you see there is the potential to be an excellent multitasker with this planet.

Health and diet are other terrains connected to Mercury. This planet can get you to think more seriously about taking care of your mind, body, and spirit. Trying to convince others to do this for themselves can be of interest to you. You may even become interested in a health-oriented type of profession. Practicing a regular exercise routine to keep your mind and body in shape is a favorite way Mercury likes to go to work for you. Developing discipline regarding your diet is another use of this planet. Learning to eliminate unhealthy things from your daily eating habits is part of the discriminating talent offered by this very insightful planet.

Your passion to get a job done right is part of the Mercury package. This planet can motivate you to learn new job skills.

Your determination to finish what you start with great accuracy can be traced back to Mercury's world. Tenacious attention to detail guides you with painstaking effort from one step to the next. Sensing what to remove to make a job run more smoothly is another feature provided by Mercury.

Mercury helps you to tune in to your tendency toward negative thinking and points the way to changing this pattern. This planet stimulates your thoughts to shift to a more positive mental approach. Ingenuity comes in bunches thanks to this mental giant of the sky. There may even be negative thoughts that have been in your mind for years. The Mercury influence can teach you how to transcend this tendency. It may take some rugged determination, but with persistence you can do this.

Communicating ideas is a major part of Mercury's world and what it can do for you. Maintaining clear communication with friends and lovers is a big purpose of this planet. Mercury assists you in getting ideas across to others. Becoming a better listener is just as important in communicating with others. You become more admired when you show you are paying attention to what those closest to you in life are saying. Retaining this information for later use is another gift of this mentally adept Mercurial energy.

How you perceive the world is linked in a big way to Mercury. Your instinct to enlarge your worldview could be a catalyst to open new creative doors of opportunity for yourself. This may spark stimulating relationships with others that keep life interesting. Knowing what has worked for you in the past to keep you mentally centered and making sure you continue to make use of this awareness is another Mercury trait. So you see, there is no end to how this mentally invigorating planet will continue to open your eyes to new insight.

Your Sun Sign, Your Sign Element, and Mercury Retrograde: A Dynamic Triad

In my 2010 book *Sun Signs and Past Lives*, I described the four elements as found in nature, which are fire, earth, air, and water. Your Sun sign is associated with one of these four elements, as you will discover in the following sections. Because it is part of an element, your Sun sign will react in a unique way to a Mercury retrograde. This does not mean you will always make the same choices or react to every Mercury retrograde in the same manner. The element discussions that follow are meant to be a general guide to help you tune in to a Mercury retrograde. This combination of your Sun sign and element join with the Mercury retrograde to offer you new insights. The three combine into a powerful perception triad that is there to help you make better informed choices.

Each element is essential for survival and finding harmony. The psychologist Carl Jung identified four psychological functions, which are emotion, intellect, sensation (as in the physical senses), and intuition. Each of these functions corresponds to one of the four elements. The emotion function is similar to the fire element as found in astrology. There are three astrological fire signs, which are Aries, Leo, and Sagittarius. The intellect function is associated with the astrological air signs, which are Gemini, Libra, and Aquarius. The sensation function, such as taste and touch, matches the experiential needs of the earth signs, which are Taurus, Virgo, and Capricorn. The intuition function is linked to the feeling nature of the water signs, which are Cancer, Scorpio, and Pisces.

Each of us in reality is somewhat of a mixture of the four elements in our psychological nature and self-expression. This becomes very evident if you get your complete astrological chart done based on your date, time, and place of birth. The Sun sign is a big player in terms of your need for recognition and desire to show the world your abilities. You may already be very knowledgeable of the dominant elements in your own astrological chart. If you are new to astrology, just knowing your Sun sign will tell you which element trinity you belong to. It is good to be aware of your Sun sign element when Mercury is retrograde. It will give you an idea of how you might react to this three-week retrograde time period and ways to adjust and survive more harmoniously. What follows are brief descriptions of how your Sun sign and elemental disposition interact with a Mercury retrograde.

The Fire Signs (Aries, Leo, Sagittarius) and Mercury Retrograde

If your Sun sign is a member of the fire element, then your usual fast-pace way of moving may feel like it has hit an unusual slowdown as the Mercury retrograde time period starts. Don't be too startled by this. It may seem as if life is sending you messages to think before you leap, which could be quite different from your normal way of doing business. Taking action impulsively might be your favorite way of meeting the present and future. You would rather have had a job done yesterday than plod through it today. Patience is often the best strategy for a fire sign during this testy Mercury cycle. If you are spinning in circles and not getting done what is needed, try focusing on what you can control. Or better yet, think of it as redirecting your energy. Restlessness will distract you. So be sure to exercise, whether you are walking, running, walking the dog, doing yard work, or engaging in other physical activities. Doing this might have a centering effect and get you back on track toward goals or projects. If you know how to meditate and it works for you, then try this as well. A fiery soul like you may need to stop, take a deep breath, and make sure you are clear about what you think you need. Pausing has its payoff in terms of keeping you from having to repeat actions done during Mercury retrograde. Delaying instant gratification might be wisdom you will appreciate later once Mercury turns direct. Courage to believe in yourself and to develop follow-through is a reward from thinking positive during Mercury retrograde.

If your Sun sign is fiery Aries (March 20–April 19), your tendency to take immediate action might feel somewhat restrained during Mercury retrograde. Don't get discouraged. This three-week period of time could be teaching you to formulate a better strategy before putting a plan into motion. You don't necessarily have to back away from a goal. Mercury in its retrograde movement could just be coaxing you to be decisive with a twist of looking before you leap.

If your Sun sign is fiery Leo (July 22–August 22), the rugged determination you possess to push through obstacles may influence you to rethink your use of willpower. You may be required during a Mercury retrograde to redirect your energy in a more productive way. You may have a good goal in mind but might not need to force an outcome. You may find clearer insight by being flexible and adaptable.

If your Sun sign is fiery Sagittarius (November 21–December 21), I can tell you from my own experience as a Sagittarius that it could help not to move in too many directions at once during a Mercury retrograde. You can still be mentally curious, and you don't have to completely resist the urge to travel in more than one direction at a time. Just don't try to promise more than you can deliver. Mercury retrograde will guide you to be mentally objective and realistic in getting your goals accomplished. Patience may be the road to harmony.

The Air Signs (Gemini, Libra, Aquarius) and Mercury Retrograde

If your Sun sign is a member of the air element, your mental tenacity may go into a tailspin when the Mercury retrograde time period begins. Those fast and sharp perceptions might seem somewhat more clouded than usual. Don't panic! It is the universe's way of sending you a message to rethink your options. Look at this as an opportunity to look deeper into a situation rather than torturing yourself over the details. You don't appreciate having your time wasted by having to repeatedly explain yourself to others. Try to prepare for some individuals needing you to communicate in simple ways to get your thinking across to them. This happens often under the gaze of a Mercury retrograde. This communication giant of the sky may have a better plan for you. When it goes direct, you will find out what this might be or you may have a bigger vision of your next moves toward a goal. Your nervous system may feel electrified during Mercury's backward orbit. Things could go smoother if you stick to a routine. Then again, if the same everyday way of operating is making your mind feel dull, you might need to step out and do something unique to stimulate your creative thinking. By doing this, the good news is that when Mercury proceeds to go direct, you will hit the ground running, ready to embrace a new opportunity.

If your Sun sign is airy Gemini (May 20–June 20), a Mercury retrograde could turn your logic upside down a bit more than usual. Don't worry. Since you are a Mercury-ruled Sun sign, there is a better than even chance that you will land on your feet. You do have somewhat of an advantage over the other signs, having a natural affinity with Mercury, since it rules your Sun sign. To get the most out of this three-week time period, it may require not panicking if a plan goes awry when you first attempt to put it into motion. You may find that plan B will be the right one. The key is to think in terms of options. You were born under a sign that detests being pinned down to one way of looking at things, so during a Mercury retrograde, remember to make use of one of your best tools, which is ingenuity.

If your Sun sign is airy Libra (September 22–October 22), your natural tendency to weigh decisions carefully may be thrown a curve ball during Mercury retrograde. The scales may be difficult to balance the way you like them. Don't despair. If you remain mentally centered, you will find your way through the fog. Clarity might come through sharing ideas with those closest to you. You thrive on teamwork, so let it work for you.

Mercury retrograde tests your mental fortitude to believe in your own opinions. Be an active listener, but don't forget to take firm steps to allow your goals to manifest.

If your Sun sign is airy Aquarius (January 20–February 19), the built-in GPS navigation system in your mind is challenged by a Mercury retrograde to stay on course to complete your goals. Despite your usual stamina to carry out a plan, it may seem like you are climbing up a steep hill more than usual. Your mental fortitude to push your way through an obstacle is always a close companion. The trick is not forcing the outcome of situations. Waiting for your unique insights to aid you in making clear decisions will test your patience but will prove to be worth the wait. A deepening of your thought processes can occur during a Mercury retrograde, which becomes more obvious after the planet moves direct.

The Earth Signs (Taurus, Virgo, Capricorn) and Mercury Retrograde

If your Sun sign is a member of the earth element, your pragmatic need to have your business in order can meet with a sudden jolt when the Mercury retrograde cycle gets started. An unexpected bill might come your way, or a delay in finishing a project that normally runs like clockwork. Your desire to see efficiency in your actions can be confusing if the details start falling apart. If you force things to happen, it will lead to frustration. This does not mean you need to give up on a plan. You probably just need to be more flexible in your thinking, as this is the key to staying happy. Even your closest friends will like you more if you appear to flow with changing circumstances. Mercury moving backward has a way of making even the most thought-out agendas require some reworking. This mischievous planet sometimes throws in a monkey wrench just to see how you react. Don't despair. Everything will likely fall back into place when this fast-moving celestial wanderer moves direct again, which will delight you. It may be that you have business to complete during this retrograde. That's fine. Just be prepared to make any necessary adjustments to make your life more rewarding. There really is a method to the madness of a Mercury retrograde cycle. Your focusing power may surprise you during a Mercury retrograde. Your determination to be a success is renewed.

If your Sun sign is earthy Taurus (April 19–May 20), a Mercury retrograde will lead you to question your current way of staying mentally focused on goals. You may not feel that you need to make any changes. Then again, if your usual way of operating is interfered with by this three-week retrograde cycle, you may need to formulate a new plan. Making quick changes is not typically a favorite way to move for Taurus. Mercury retrograde will likely find you analyzing business decisions even more carefully than you normally do. Stay clear of being overly stubborn and people will like you more. The best thing to do if you are not sure about making a major choice is not to make one during Mercury retrograde. Listen to your inner voice. Mercury retrograde can actually help you clarify a decision that has been puzzling you for quite some time. Be open to receiving solid advice from others and life will go more smoothly.

If your Sun sign is earthy Virgo (August 22–September 22), a Mercury retrograde will instill a passion for looking at details. You are one of the Mercury-ruled signs, which gives you a natural connection to the Mercury wavelength. Try not to go overboard with perfection. It is okay to make a mistake. You can correct missteps later. Too much worry about situations that you can't change will get you into trouble. This retrograde cycle allows you to work in a very focused way. Your insights into decisions may become crystal clear. Try to find techniques to help you relax. This opens up your creative vitality and empowers your mind, body, and spirit immensely.

If your Sun sign is earthy Capricorn (December 21–January 20), a Mercury retrograde will entice you not to feel like you have to be in complete control of all aspects of your life. Why? So some new information can penetrate your mind. Don't resist new learning during a Mercury retrograde. There may be some clues during the three-week cycle as to how to handle a situation. Remember to be harder on a problem than on people, including yourself. Pace yourself to avoid burnout. Resting at regular intervals will give you greater mental energy. It is very true during this planetary retrograde period that when you reveal your deepest thoughts, it brings your loved ones closer. "Don't fear change" is a strong Mercury message. Some variety in your life refreshes your thinking.

The Water Signs (Cancer, Scorpio, Pisces) and Mercury Retrograde

If your Sun sign is a member of the water element, your emotions may be more distracting than usual as the Mercury retrograde cycle begins. Your reliable mental perceptions could evaporate right in the middle of getting a goal accomplished.

Why? There is a tendency for emotional and mental energies to conflict in a Mercury retrograde, which might cause inaction. Your natural instinct is to plan and get things done, but you may feel like you are treading water. This is a good time to call a timeout. Formulating a better way to move forward may help. Then again, you may need to take a risk and push yourself to pursue a new goal anyway. You may not be able to sit and wait for Mercury to turn direct before finishing a job. It is better to move forward if you must and give yourself permission to make changes later. This is one way to get your mind and your emotions on the same page. Your creative power might pleasantly surprise you during this time period and be powerfully released after Mercury turns direct. Your courage to believe in your talents pays off. Mercury retrograde sometimes acts as a catalyst to deepen your intuitive energy and helps you to find ways to put new insights into action. Your self-esteem rises to high levels, helping you attract the abundance you need to be happy.

If your Sun sign is watery Cancer (June 20–July 22), a Mercury retrograde might begin with some mental static. Don't worry about that. It may be that you are bringing emotional issues into the retrograde cycle that feel like they are getting tossed around over and over again in a clothes dryer with no result. If you stay focused on your key objectives, there is a better than average chance that your thoughts will straighten themselves out. It is possible that you could hit the ground running at the beginning of a Mercury retrograde cycle and never stop for the entire three weeks. Your creative instincts and physical energy stay centered if you remain grounded. If you are having difficulty focusing, you may need to meditate or indulge in activities that relax your mind. You likely prefer situations where you can predict their probable outcome before entering them. This preference is magnified during a Mercury retrograde. As a general rule, make extra sure you know what you are getting into on the business and relationship levels during a Mercury retrograde. This will save you time, money, and energy. Think positive. It will be the key to open the doors to harmony.

If your Sun sign is watery Scorpio (October 22–November 21), a Mercury retrograde will encourage you to deeply process all of your main plans that you brought into the cycle. Your ability to delve beneath the surface of things gets a boost from Mercury retrograde. The passion to study a subject or excel at a job may intensify. Be careful not to needlessly worry over details that won't really give you a different result in solving a problem. Channel your energy into productive objectives rather than being hijacked by negative thoughts. Letting others know how you honestly feel about situations keeps communication clearer. Mastering new skills could allow for greater options in your work world. Your business insights can be marketed in new ways. Clarifying your short- or long-range goals may be a key priority. Your problem-solving capability comes in handy to deal with challenges you face.

If your Sun sign is watery Pisces (February 19–March 20), a Mercury retrograde might help you become more objective about a situation. The mental energy of Mercury helps you distance yourself from your anxiety about a circumstance. Business and relationship decisions could find clarity during this cycle. Remember not to assume that others can read your mind. Talking not only will keep you on the same page with people but will also help you maintain a feeling of being on top of your main plans. Denial is probably the key thing to watch out for during a Mercury retrograde. Be honest with yourself. Is a life experience delivering what it was supposed to offer? You don't have to change it during this three-week retrograde time period, but be ready to act on your insights. Your creative power can build and be expressed at the same time during a Mercury retrograde. Keep believing in your ability and good things will come your way. A positive outlook attracts good fortune.

Surviving a Mercury Retrograde
Through Rewiring Your Perceptions

Retrograde Mercury Survival Toolbox

- Think positive.
- Review details, but don't obsess over them.
- Rethink what you are trying to communicate.
- Try not to worry too much about outcomes.
- Be open to change and new learning.

Mercury is the most famous of the retrograde planets. Mercury goes retrograde three or four times a year. Each Mercury retrograde lasts for a time span of twenty to twenty-four days. Whatever your Sun sign may be, these few weeks sometimes feel like an eternity if you are struggling to keep your thinking clear. You can find yourself anxiously waiting each day for the clarity to move forward with big decisions or even the smallest of plans.

What follows are survival tips to help you better make sense of a Mercury retrograde when you are in one.

Think of this as your opportunity to decode the Mercury messages being sent to you. Hopefully the tips offered here will give you that extra edge to confidently and insightfully deal with the three- to four-week Mercury retrograde when it comes your way a few times a year. Be patient with yourself. Remember that the rest of the world is probably dealing with many of the same issues you are having to endure. There is a light at the end of the tunnel. You can live your life with a minimum of trouble and anxiety by making use of these survival tips.

Tips for Surviving Mercury Retrograde
Tip 1 for Surviving Mercury Retrograde:
Let Go of Perfection

The attention-to-detail tendencies embedded in Mercury energy can grow wildly obsessive during this planet's retrograde cycle. It can be hard to know when to stop trying to perfect a project. You may find yourself going over and over the same worries in your head. Problems tend to magnify quickly during this planet's retrograde motion. The powers of analysis that are wonderful to put to use when Mercury is direct can become troublesome if you can't stop worrying.

What is the solution to making this perfection tendency not be problematic? You need to give yourself a new direction to focus on. Compartmentalizing is one way out of this dilemma. In other words, put your energy into something that is not making you feel crazy and filled with anxiety. It might come down to an activity that gives you more of a feeling of being in control. You have to tell yourself that experiencing endless anxiety over making something perfect is not good for your mental or physical health.

What you are attempting to do is to break the spell of wanting to be too perfect. If you are too concerned about pleasing others, then realize that you will not make everybody happy with even your best effort. In the end, you may be happier just trying to please yourself. Even making something into your idea of perfect is not going to make you happy. This can become a recurring worry for you with each Mercury retrograde if you don't break the pattern. Learn to accept that your best effort is good enough.

My favorite image of an individual's yearning for perfection is symbolized in the sculpture the Pietà, created by the famous artist Michelangelo. Supposedly he created this depiction of the Crucifixion by carving away what did not belong in his vision of the sculpture. In other words, he removed piece by piece and in painstaking detail the superfluous qualities until all that remained was a magnificent, breathtaking masterpiece.

You may find it challenging to stay focused consistently during a Mercury retrograde. Your creative power will rise and your self-confidence emanate when you make peace with a compulsive drive to be perfect, so it is vital to find ways to let go of an over-attachment to perfecting an end result. There will come a point with practice to realize when enough is enough.

Tip 2 for Surviving Mercury Retrograde: When in Doubt, Think Positive

In David Baird's book *Where Cats Meditate*, there is a saying by Buddha: "Be vigilant; guard your mind against negative thoughts." It is good to remind yourself about this Buddha quote during a Mercury retrograde. Mercury is a wonderful planet when it arouses your brain to think with inspiration, but there is the chance that old problems and issues could haunt you during a Mercury retrograde. It is as though they have come out of the closet. This might occur after being contacted by someone from your past, or it may be more of a hidden insecurity about a situation that is revisiting your thoughts. Suddenly feeling less on top of your game may come as an unpleasant surprise. Mental confusion can get stirred up by a Mercury retrograde until you steady yourself again.

The best cure is to think positive. Don't get distracted by what might be going wrong. Get out and do things with people who make you feel upbeat and more alive. Stimulating your mind through indulging in your favorite subjects or hobbies is a smart thing to do.

Mercury retrograde occasionally spins us into what appears to be an odd direction or one that is out of our comfort zone. Our normal way of thinking gets a jolt. It may be hard to believe, but this could be a good thing. You are being guided to rethink your options. Your perceptions may eventually sharpen to help you see your way out of the confusion. What results is a fresh new insight. Your mental energy is stimulated to new heights. A feeling of rebirth could seem worth the temporary discomfort brought on by the retrograde cycle. This can be an altered way of perceiving the world that is very much to your benefit. Accenting the positive attracts the good luck and opportunities you seek.

You may be surprised to realize that it takes a lot less energy to look at life through positive eyes than ones that expect bad things to occur. If you give yourself permission to anticipate that life will be good to you, it really is wisdom that pays big dividends. You will attract a more abundant life. With some practice, you really can retrain your mind to think positive. With a lot of repetition, you could escape from being caught in negative thinking. Mercury retrograde is a great time to start putting this new thinking into practice. Repeating a positive message in many ways has even more power during this retrograde cycle.

Tip 3 for Surviving Mercury Retrograde: Be Open to Change

Being flexible is a great way to handle a Mercury retrograde. Change is inevitable. People will warn you against moving forward haphazardly during Mercury's backward cycle. This may appear like wise advice. There can be a strong temptation to hold on to old behaviors even though in reality you know they won't bring you what you need. However, taking the risk of adjusting your goals or plans for the future could be a good idea. Making use of the reflective energy of this retrograde celestial wanderer to rethink a strategy is displaying wisdom. Diversification is Mercury's calling card. Finding a new option can be the road to success. You won't lose your focus by considering new solutions to a problem. It will feel like a breath of fresh air to consider a new job, a new subject to study, or a new direction to move in. Shaking up those old thought patterns can be very liberating. It frees you to develop a wonderful new outlook.

What you are already accustomed to doing in life may be challenging to leave behind. A willingness to at least consider a change in circumstances might be the path to reinvent yourself. When you first open up to a change, it may not be obvious that it could bring you increased happiness or rewards. Letting go of a comfort zone to pursue a new opportunity often opens the door to even more possibilities. This is the way your luck could change during a Mercury retrograde.

Change is a way to unlock the grip of the past—or at least the part of the past you may need to leave behind to feel a sense of liberation. Gaining freedom from limiting situations is like getting a new lease on life. After accepting a new life direction, your mind, body, and spirit may be asking you something like, "What took you so long?" So you see, it is possible even during a Mercury retrograde that trading one life experience for a new one could be just the prescription for a happier you.

Tip 4 for Surviving Mercury Retrograde: Give and Receive Criticism Carefully

During a Mercury retrograde, being criticized feels worse than usual for most people. Criticism has a way of working its way into the deepest recesses of your mind. It hurts more than usual. Why? Because this retrograde cycle lowers your resistance to fighting off negative energy unless you are determined to resist it with all of your mental alertness. If you are receiving criticism of your work or something that means a lot to you, it can interfere with your self-confidence. The best thing to do is to take what benefits you from the criticism and push the rest out of your mind. It might hurt a little, but there is the possibility that you can convert critical feedback into an asset, especially during a Mercury retrograde. There is a lot of power in a retrograde to empower yourself by rising above negative comments. You can learn to toughen up enough to push through the remarks of those who don't have your best interests in mind.

During this retrograde time period, Mercury can be trying to help you develop a more discerning eye as to whom to trust regarding criticism. You may get quite good at quickly perceiving if someone is offering valid and constructive criticism or perhaps is just trying to make your life miserable. You can become an expert at spotting negative energy that is coming at you and learn to get out of the way before it has a full impact. This is not running away as much as protecting yourself to maintain your mental health.

Be careful when giving others criticism during a Mercury retrograde. It is helpful to show that you are really trying to be supportive through your words rather than only being critical. Your suggestions carry more power and intensity than they might ordinarily during this retrograde. To keep the communication clear, be aware of the impact you are going to have on someone when being critical. Saying something positive first opens the door to someone being more receptive to your ideas. People will be much more open to your suggestions or insights about their behavior if they feel you are really on their side. This keeps the tension to a minimum during a retrograde. Communication can run wild during a Mercury retrograde. It can seem like a tornado suddenly hit with no warning. You may not have even intended to come on so strong in correcting what someone was doing or saying. Words may easily be taken the wrong way. It may seem like someone heard something completely different coming out of your mouth, judging by the reaction you are getting. So be a little more careful if you want someone to treat you differently or you want their actions to change. There is a greater likelihood that a person will respond more harmoniously if you express some empathy for their situation. You don't need to act like you want to walk a mile in their shoes, but it helps to take a step in showing you are hearing them.

Tip 5 for Surviving Mercury Retrograde: Avoid Communication Breakdowns

Communicating your ideas so people understand them is a challenge during a Mercury retrograde. Getting on the same page takes extra work but is very achievable. Don't be surprised if you need to say the same thing three different ways to get your point across to someone. For example, you could be required to explain more clearly than usual why you want to return an item for a refund. People might look at you like you are speaking a foreign language even though your words and ideas seem more than reasonable to you. Making your ideas understandable so there can be a meeting of the minds may mean you need to listen to someone else with greater concentration. Don't get upset if you are not understood during your first try. Rushing to make a point may delay getting what you need. Take your time, and you may need to talk a little slower. People don't always process information as quickly during a Mercury retrograde.

Formulating a strategy ahead of time as to what you want to get across to others is a good idea during a Mercury retrograde. This will allow you to get in sync with the energy flow of Mercury. It will help keep you from being overly aggressive in pushing to get your own way. You will appear more assertive and under control with a little prep work done ahead of time. Your impulse to overreact to others will be lessened as well.

The closer you are to a person emotionally, the more intense communication can become over touchy issues. This communication voltage tends to multiply during a Mercury retrograde when you are trying to discuss an area of conflict with a lover, close friend, child, or business colleague. Communication can get into a fog before you realize it. There is an objective feature to Mercury in the communication process that helps reduce the tension when negotiating with someone. The trick is remembering to make use of it. As said earlier, it helps to slow yourself down when trying to score your points with someone in a dispute. Take a few deep breaths or make yourself listen for a few moments to the other person's point of view, even if you strongly disagree with it. The idea is to take some of the heated emotion out of the dispute. It is almost like finding ways to stay centered in the midst of a crisis. With practice, you can do it.

Picking the right time to discuss a touchy subject is just as vital to the success of getting the outcome or resolution you hope to reach with a person. If one or both of you are exhausted, it is likely a bad time to talk about an emotionally charged topic. It could be like setting a match to gasoline. So choosing a more opportune time for a serious powwow is wise. Keep the talk lighter until then.

Tip 6 for Surviving Mercury Retrograde: Be Careful What Documents You Sign

Signing contracts and other types of important documents is best done with careful consideration during a Mercury retrograde. You need to make sure that the commitment of time and money is worth it. If you are not certain, the wisest policy is to wait for Mercury to go direct. Patience is the best strategy if it is possible to put off signing on the dotted line. There are those times when you can't afford to put off a major decision. Accepting a job offer could be in your best interest or even buying a house during a Mercury retrograde. Just be sure there is no way to delay taking action until after the Mercury retrograde.

If your instincts are telling you to get a second opinion about a situation, then you should do so. Details are easy to miss and are sometimes hidden during a Mercury retrograde. It may be that a person is concealing them from you. Retrogrades are great for carefully reviewing any major decision. Another person's insights could prove very beneficial. This could prevent you from hiring the wrong person to do a job for you. You may need to wear your detective hat during some Mercury retrogrades and do the right research.

If you do decide to throw caution to the wind, be sure you dot all of the i's and cross all of the t's, as the old saying goes. It is good to be aware of the consequences of signing any written agreement ahead of time. Read the fine print. If you are dealing with a salesperson and have a bad feeling about a deal, trust your instincts and wait. There is probably a better opportunity right around the corner. This is often the case once a Mercury retrograde is over.

Even a job offer or promotion may have some hidden responsibilities you are not being told about during an interview. The place of employment might have large problems that will be extremely stressful to walk into. It might be wise to talk to someone who knows something about the company you are considering joining before signing on to a new life direction. If you do accept, be sure you are being awarded the right pay to make the change rewarding.

I have signed contracts with organizations to go out of town to do a workshop that would take place during a Mercury retrograde. Before I go on such journeys, I try to be extra prepared and make sure to take what I need with me. My experiences during those occasions went fine. There are simply times when you will be faced with important challenges during a Mercury retrograde and you will decide that you must make the commitment. The main message here is to be as prepared as possible during a Mercury retrograde cycle.

Tip 7 for Surviving Mercury Retrograde: Discover Your Inventive Insights

Think of a Mercury retrograde as an opportunity to reinvent your thought processes. It might simply be a tweak in your perceptions that gives you the clarity to solve an old problem. You might be surfing the Internet and see an article that helps you see your way out of a situation. While browsing in a bookstore, you may find a book that provides great answers to a question you have. The wonderful timing cannot be denied. It does require you to keep your mind alert so this retrograde cycle can be your best friend. There is an inventive streak in the Mercury influence on your mind. You might be surprised at how the universe can work with your mind in a synchronistic way to bring you exactly what you need to gain new insights.

When you relax and try to lessen your anxiety during a Mercury retrograde, interesting and exciting things can occur. This approach paves the way to perceive a new path to success that you may have overlooked. Think of it as solving a puzzle. Mercury can deepen your research ability. When probing for a solution, you can find a favorable response if you possess an upbeat attitude.

Try to be open to alternative methods of doing things. Thinking outside of the box is certainly within your grasp during a Mercury retrograde. Einstein said that insanity was doing the same thing over and over again and expecting different results. Slipping out from under the hold of your past analytical tendencies may not be as difficult as you imagine it to be. It may take working in a different setting. If you always work indoors, try doing so outside. If you are in the habit of working from a home office, try a coffee house or other type of location. If you are doing projects from a company office, try to work at home or in a place that takes you out of the same mental framework. If you need an ocean view or the mountains, go for it. The idea here is to activate your inventive thoughts.

Your work skills can get a boost. This retrograde period might enhance your learning ability. All it takes is a little focus and good things can happen for you. If you are preparing a sales pitch or trying to advertise a product, you may discover an innovative approach. You could tune in to communicating information to others in a unique way. The teacher, advisor, and networker in you are emphasized. Verbal and writing talents can find new creative outlets.

Tip 8 for Surviving Mercury Retrograde: Travel Will Help You Process Your Thoughts

Mercury is a travel planet, so if you are on the move, this planet helps you to better assimilate the information being transmitted to you during its retrograde cycle. This does not have to be a long journey. Short walks or drives around town work just fine. This is a good way to rethink a plan of action to make sure you have all of the details straight in your mind. My own theory is that the forward movement helps fool your mind into thinking that Mercury is moving direct or at least gives you the sensation of advancing in energy.

It is easy to let your nervous system get out of control during Mercury retrograde, which can distort your thought processes and cloud your mental clarity. Travel is a possible healing remedy to keep you clearheaded. It can help you see the bigger picture regarding a situation or problem. Getting away from your living or work environment even for short periods of time may be the key to seeing your way back to clarity. Your creativity could find rejuvenation through travel.

If you are feeling mentally depressed or are just not feeling like your usual positive self, then travel might be the solution to getting you back on the right track. If you fear a new situation or a situation that seems out of your control, travel may allow you to see it in a new light. A friend once sent me a cartoon with a bird thinking it was locked in a cage. The sad bird had its head down and was looking straight down at the bars of the cage. A little bit to the left and right, the bars were missing. The bird only had to look to its left or right to see its way out of being locked up. Travel can point you in a direction to see more alternatives to your current problems and predicaments. It is a type of yoga or meditation that relaxes the mind during a Mercury retrograde.

Our minds are affected by places we visit or where we currently reside. During certain Mercury retrogrades, a person can be helped to get past an issue or gain clarity about their life path by changing locations. This could involve a move or going somewhere on vacation. If you are feeling stuck, there is a possibility during a Mercury retrograde to reverse this trend by traveling to a different location. Mercury is a travel planet, so you could stimulate your brain to think more positively or with a new perspective by exploring another locale. It is amazing what a change of venue might do for you if you are trying to reinvent your thinking.

There is even the possibility that a past-life issue might be interfering with your current life happiness. You may feel an urge to travel to a particular place and wonder why this is even occurring. There could be a past-life memory linked to this other location blocking you from releasing your creative flow. It might be that traveling to the location to which you feel drawn will help you resolve an inner state of confusion or a question you very much want answered. The energy of this other place may help you see a situation with greater clarity. Visiting this other place might bring you to a new level of understanding. There is a lot of magic contained in a Mercury retrograde that could work with you in mysterious ways.

Tip 9 for Surviving Mercury Retrograde:
Don't Let Your Routines Limit Your Creative Thinking

Mercury is the planet that encourages you to develop routines. Everyone needs a sense of order to keep their life organized. Staying with the same way of doing things during a Mercury retrograde has its advantages and disadvantages. It helps you stay focused on your usual way of operating. Focusing on familiar things and allowing your thoughts to stay in their comfort zone helps you avoid mental confusion and indecision. You could be working on a project and don't want to get out of the current flow you are enjoying. A Mercury retrograde can give you the sensation that you are moving against the current for a few weeks, so following your same routine might help you push through any obstacles in your path. It is that consistency in your daily habits that can give you a reliable structure to get through each day with a sense of order. During certain Mercury retrogrades, this might be the path to harmony and inner peace. You will get a sense of satisfaction in completing what you set out to do.

It is possible that staying with the same routines during a Mercury retrograde cycle won't work each day of the time period, or it could be that a different experience during some of the days in the retrograde cycle will show you how to get the most out of this time period. You may need to get out of the repetitive routines to stimulate your mental spark. Mercury is a very mental planet, as it does rule Gemini, a quick-witted sign. Its co-rulership of Virgo does influence us to adopt routines, which is a natural influence of this pragmatic earth sign. The Gemini side of Mercury that enjoys darting off toward new and innovative ideas could show your need to escape from routines if you feel trapped in them. Your mind may be dulled by doing the same thing every day. Even taking a different route to a job or a class can give you new insight. It may be the way to drop a negative feeling for the day. The key message here is that variety could just be the spice of life you require to give your eyes a fresh new life perspective. You may surprise yourself by making even a slight change to your normal way of doing things each day. Your life does not need to be in a big state of flux to snap you out of a mental funk. Just a slight alteration could be all you need to keep your life moving forward the way you like it.

Tip 10 for Surviving Mercury Retrograde: Keep a Mercury Retrograde Journal

You may not be a writer, but keeping a few notes to yourself on how you deal with Mercury retrogrades could be a very informative learning experience. You may already be someone who keeps a journal or even writes a blog on an ongoing basis. Even if you do not ordinarily keep track of your experiences, there is a chance that it might prove rewarding during a Mercury retrograde. Why? You may get some insight into a situation, or it could even help you better prepare for a future Mercury retrograde by realizing how you were able to deal with a previous one. You don't have to write down a lot of information. Keeping a few notes to yourself might be enough. Having a history on hand will allow you to look back with more confidence, knowing you were able to get through previous

Mercury retrogrades productively. If you struggled in certain ways, you can see this as learning from past experiences.

You may prove to be your own therapist. Mercury is a great teacher, allowing you to reflect on your own thinking and your communications with others. You can feel more affected by what others say to you during a Mercury retrograde. Putting into a journal your reactions to input from other people could help you clarify how you might want to respond to them. A journal may become a valuable asset as a way to empower you. Your creative ideas can benefit from this recordkeeping in a written format during your Mercury retrograde experience.

Mercury retrograde gives you an extra edge to be a detective or researcher. Think of this as probing into your own thought patterns as a method to gain insight into life situations. This could be a valuable resource throughout your life. There is a natural introspective influence brought on by a Mercury retrograde. You can use this influence to analyze your inner motivations, or better yet, to help you determine a course of action to stay centered and happy during a Mercury retrograde.

Tip 11 for Surviving Mercury Retrograde: *Avoid Dual Exhaustion Burnout*

Your mind can easily speed up during Mercury retrograde. Our mental filters seem to get on overload faster than when Mercury is moving direct. It is as though the mind's defenses to keep out useless or distracting information are not as easy to manage, so it is wise to give yourself permission to take a timeout and relax. With practice, you can get good at eliminating information in a way that is similar to protecting yourself against spam in your email. But you do have to be vigilant.

Mercury is always ready to open the door for you to learn new information. Moving in multiple directions is a great temptation and keeps life stimulating. You may get burned out if you try to bite off more than you can chew. Be careful how much extra responsibility you take on during a Mercury retrograde. The fatigue factor could suddenly multiply in ways you had not counted on. This does not mean you won't be able to tackle a tough job. Just know your boundaries in estimating how much time and energy you have. Your brain can become so excited by new information that it may not warn you that perhaps you can't possibly get a job done in the allotted time. It is easy to overestimate your energy levels to the point of getting burned out.

A Mercury retrograde can pull at you strongly in two different directions. There is an east/west or north/south type of energy that can spin your brain in a completely different direction like the force of a tornado. You may not even realize this is happening until well after you wind up in a completely different place than where you started. Your mind could suddenly speed up from zero to sixty because you are thinking about too many things at once. You might forget to slow down before you lose all of your momentum to get a plan finished or maybe even started.

There is good news here. Mercury retrograde is an excellent time period in which to multitask. Mercury can guide you to stay mentally sharp while taking care of business on multiple fronts. You only need to get good at warding off useless information and too many worries that are competing for your attention. Try thinking in terms of doing one thing well to reset your focus in a productive direction.

Tip 12 for Surviving Mercury Retrograde: See the Big Picture

There is an old saying of "not seeing the forest for the trees." During a Mercury retrograde, it is easy to get lost in the details and lose sight of your bigger objectives. There is the possibility of feeling bombarded by outside stimuli, causing your sense of direction to become foggy. You may need to constantly remind yourself of what your overall purpose is during the few weeks of this retrograde time period. You may need to keep this in front of you at regular intervals so you don't lose your way. It is important not to panic. If you have a difficult time maintaining your train of thought during a Mercury retrograde, you can always wait for Mercury to move direct. But what if you can't wait? Then slow down just enough to get a hold on your main objectives. Keep life simple and less aggravating. You will waste much less time and perceive life as being more rewarding. If you learn not to let anxiety get the best of you, then it won't be hard to successfully complete a goal.

Sometimes just staying centered and reasonable with yourself will keep you on target. If you obsess over any one detail, it can throw you way off course and you will stop focusing on your main goals. To keep your longer-range hopes and dreams in focus, remember to keep them alive in your mind. Often the details will fall into place when you are happy and healthy. You might need to be your own cheerleader and coach at times. Keep telling yourself you can finish what you start. Repeating positive mantras or even posting them on your refrigerator are ways to maintain a broader and upbeat perspective. It helps to have a person in your life who can help you stay focused on a plan. Envisioning the final result allows the fire to stay alive and keep you motivated to achieve your aspirations.

Tip 13 for Surviving Mercury Retrograde: Remember to Speak

Quiet contemplation is a good method to keep your thoughts straight and your mind clear of debris. Mercury retrograde offers as much of a reminder to reflect than if you lived in a monastery. Where this can be challenging is in your closest personal relationships. You may live too much in your mind, assuming people can read your thoughts. Unless you have a completely psychic connection with someone, you must communicate. Even then, it helps to verbalize your needs and expectations. Otherwise you will be perceived as living in your own world. Your closeness will disappear. Intimacy with a lover is hard to achieve if you don't say what is on your mind. It is okay if you need some space from someone, but be sure not to use this as an excuse to hide your true ideas and feelings.

If you are dealing with someone during a Mercury retrograde who is concealing their feelings and not being honest, you may need to address this. A few weeks can seem a lot longer if a cloud of confusion settles over the relationship. Breaking the ice takes a bit of courage but is well worth it if it will dissolve the distance between you and a lover or family member. It is not as difficult to be the initiator of communication as your mind may be telling you it is. Once you get started, you could surprise yourself with how much better you feel than if you had kept everything bottled up inside. The positive response you get for talking in a vibrant way can win you accolades from others.

In your business dealings, you may need to remind yourself to be more direct. Mercury retrograde could find you not promoting your ideas with as much force. If you are wanting to advertise yourself, then you may need to push forward with confidence, though it is easier said than done during this retrograde cycle. Your mind can feel like it is treading water. You would be wise to have a business confidant keep an eye on you to make sure you are not taking one step forward and then three backward. You can do the same for them, as it is possible that their own momentum has stalled somewhat. Being there for a friend or lover in the same way builds a communication rapport. The idea is to keep each other moving with momentum and, more importantly, a sense of direction.

The same could be true as far as working with coworkers, employees, or supervisors. Miscommunication is par for the course during a Mercury retrograde. You may not be on the same page with those you work with, but this can be corrected quickly. How? By making sure you make your expectations of others clear and making sure you really are hearing what is expected of you. You may imagine that the communication is flowing, but you could be assuming too much. Checking in more frequently with those in your business world is just as vital as doing this in your private life. The main message here is to talk at regular intervals with people to stay on the same page. This will help you maintain greater closeness in your personal life and make your work life more rewarding and less stressful.

Tip 14 for Surviving Mercury Retrograde:
Pay Attention to Your Health

During a Mercury retrograde, it is not uncommon for people to begin thinking about taking care of nagging health problems that they have put off. There is a health dimension to Mercury that could motivate you to look into finding a doctor or remedy that meets your health needs. Researching the right solution for you can actually go well when Mercury is moving retrograde. Even if you decide to wait to have a medical procedure done until Mercury is moving direct once again, the retrograde cycle offers an opportunity to do some research.

The retrograde period might even be a better time to consider handling a persistent health ailment than when Mercury is direct. Why? Because this is often when you are willing to slow down and deal with finding the answer to your health challenge. If you are a fast-paced type of person, this is probably especially true. Sometimes we don't realize that we need to decelerate. It is easy to be fooled into thinking that our energy levels are operating at top speed even though our body is signaling otherwise.

During Mercury retrograde, you could have a tendency to think your obligations are more important to focus on than your health. Be careful in this instance, as what starts out as a small health problem could get bigger fast. For instance, a sinus infection that is neglected could become something more serious if you are in denial. It is so easy to focus so much on work that working through an illness seems plausible. You might be under the illusion that the illness will heal itself if you ignore it. Being responsible and focused is a great thing, but not having a balance in taking care of your health could get you into trouble. It might require slowing down just enough to let your body recover from an illness, or taking the time to go to a doctor, or investigating a way to solve your health challenge.

You might want to help others so intensely that you forget to pay attention to your own health. Being a caretaker for others can be an emotional strain. If you are out of balance in paying attention to your own needs as well as those of someone else, it may wear you down.

Thoughts about your diet can surface during a Mercury retrograde. There can be digestive disturbances, especially if you are in the middle of a stressful time period. Perhaps you need to tweak what you are in the habit of eating. A busy schedule may be causing you not to have a healthy meal plan. Eating the wrong things can cause you not to have the same energy you normally enjoy. It is surprising how eating right can be good for your mental and physical well-being.

Gaining insight into a health issue is possible during a Mercury retrograde. Discovering an alternative remedy to a health problem is a possibility. It could be that you are more open to rethinking a problem and finding a new solution. It is possible that while surfing the Internet or watching a television show, you find out about another route to take in dealing with a health obstacle.

Mercury is associated with the lungs in the body. Yoga breathing or doing a type of meditation that involves listening to your breath might help keep you centered during a Mercury retrograde. If you are more of an on-the-go type of person, then exercise that gets you breathing more deeply, like jogging or taking a brisk walk, might pump up your vitality during a Mercury retrograde.

The value of a power nap should never be underestimated. This is very true if you are sleep-deprived. During a Mercury retrograde, you could even get more out of sleep. It is as though your mind is programmed to know it needs to rest. Sleep can add great vitality to mind, body, and spirit.

Tip 15 for Surviving Mercury Retrograde:
Too Much Analysis Can Cause Mental Paralysis

Mercury retrograde will put your mind into a deep analysis of details. There is no sense in denying this or telling you this is unlikely. The key thing to remember is that going over the same information in your head probably won't make it any easier to understand. Problem situations intensify under Mercury retrograde. It is not that the outer circumstances change all that much. So where does the greater tension come from? It is the internal struggle in obsessing over finding an answer. It can keep you up at night with endless worry.

Somehow you need to get good at letting go of the anxiety, because worrying does not resolve a problem anyway. This particular retrograde can get your mind to constantly sift through information to the point of making you feel dizzy. Distracting yourself into more productive outlets really helps. Remember to focus on what you can control, as it will help to neutralize an obsession with repeatedly putting the same thoughts through the sifter.

It is a gift to be able to put the details into the creative process. They are just as vital to success as the big plan. With a lot of practice, even during a Mercury retrograde you can learn to excel at knowing what needs to be deleted without causing you too much aggravation.

Think of this as being your own best friend in letting yourself off the hook. Give yourself permission to stop splitting hairs over the details. This is one time when putting off all of those details until tomorrow is a good thing. The following day you might feel refreshed and glad you had the confidence to give yourself a break.

Tip 16 for Surviving Mercury Retrograde: Make Productive Decisions in the World of Business and Career

You can't stop working on a job or running a business for three weeks while Mercury is retrograde. So how do you get through this time period successfully? Just make sure you are extra careful about what you are trying to communicate to others. If you are trying to sell products, be sure to explain things in simple terms to get your point across clearly. It might be you are training people to learn a new job, as in sharing your skills with them. Be patient. It may take someone a little longer to catch on. If you are being trained to take on a new assignment, be patient with yourself. It could require extra repetition on your part to put it all together in your head.

If you are building or working on a website, you may need to be prepared to rewrite some of the information you are presenting. Identify ahead of time the people you might be trying to reach with your information. This will minimize the rewrites. The same advice would go for any written or even visual material you are presenting. Keep a broad vision and don't forget the details. There is a tendency during a Mercury retrograde to lose an audience by not leading them carefully enough. So take your time and give people the right tempo to stay in step with you. If you are speaking in public, talk at a pace at which the audience can digest your concepts. You will need to be sure to keep everyone on the same page with you.

If you are going on an interview during a Mercury retrograde, it is likely that a second interview will be requested of you. The more prepared you are for the interview, the more smoothly it will go, especially during a Mercury retrograde. If you can make it clear why you want the job as well as knowing what it requires, you will be one step ahead of the game. Knowledge about how the company functions at a basic level puts you in the driver's seat.

If you are operating a business, you may be surprised to hear that a Mercury retrograde cycle may be a great one to re-connect with your clients/customers. I have had some of my greatest responses during this time period. A retrograde Mercury has a natural flow of bringing people back to you. It does not always work as well with new customers, but it really works with going back to previous ones in my experience.

You may find that a company that once was not interested in your job skills may change their mind during a Mercury retrograde. Their need for you could be there, so approaching them once again could work for you. It might be that the company is expanding or that someone in a position you wanted has vacated that particular job.

Research instincts can deepen during retrograde visits from Mercury. It is a good time to explore ways to make your business function better and to improve your skills. Your focusing power to find innovative ways to stimulate your imagination and to market your talents may intensify under the watchful eye of a retrograde Mercury.

Handling all of your business affairs can be done under a Mercury retrograde. Perhaps you are wanting to negotiate a better deal to purchase an item. Wear your business hat and be determined to get the price you would like. A little flexibility on your part will be in your best interest. Work for a win-win agreement and you will be more likely to find success.

Tip 17 for Surviving Mercury Retrograde:
Don't Put Off until Tomorrow What You Could Do Today

It is easy to fall into denial during a Mercury retrograde regarding whether to take action. It is easier to find excuses to delay pursuing a goal. Your mind can interpret the slower pace of this cycle as a wait-and-see attitude. You might need to give yourself a nudge to put out your best effort in getting a job done. Some deadlines just can't wait, whether you are dealing with a Mercury retrograde or not.

Don't resist a push from a friend to keep moving forward. You may be called upon to do this for someone else. Friends, lovers, or other family members might need encouraging words from you if self-doubt stands in their way.

Remember that your perceptions are somewhat skewed during this retrograde. Your mind might be in a tug of war dealing with the dilemma of "should I wait or should I go?"

Don't feel like you are alone. Everybody else is in the midst of this same challenge, whether they are showing it or not. There is really nothing to lose in moving forward with an idea. You can always backtrack and rethink a better way to proceed.

Tip 18 for Surviving Mercury Retrograde: If You Are Stuck, Ask for Help

One of the biggest mistakes people make during a Mercury retrograde is thinking they have to go it alone. So you must remember one of the key tools Mercury puts in your pocket to make use of at all times, which is communication. If you don't let others know you are experiencing extreme mental confusion, you could remain in this state of mind longer than necessary. Reach out to your friends and lovers. If needed, ask a counselor for assistance with your dilemma. You may not really want someone else to solve your problems. The talking process can put you in the driver's seat in being clearer about a decision. Just saying what is on your mind can trigger your own answer during this retrograde period.

It may be hard to imagine that spoken words have the capacity to lift you out of a dark place in your mind. Your tongue may grow silent more regularly during a Mercury retrograde when you feel stressed out. It happens to many people, so don't feel alone. But you don't have to be one of them. Think of this as a type of talking yoga. You can climb out of what feels like a deep cavern within yourself by verbalizing your inner world. It does not need to be fancy talk. The act of communicating can lead you back to a point of clarity.

You may feel too shy or embarrassed to let anyone know you are feeling trapped by a situation. Taking that first step to express yourself in words can elevate you above where you are stuck. Your communication power releases quickly after you get unglued from a mental fog. It takes some courage at times to risk looking vulnerable to others. The reward for revealing that you are feeling somewhat lost in the dark is that soon you will move quickly again into the light. The healing energy Mercury offers in the form of verbalizing your inner world is easy to forget about when you are in the middle of trying to find your own way forward. This retrograde energy has a way of helping you to penetrate right through an obstacle. You need only give yourself permission to use it.

Tip 19 for Surviving Mercury Retrograde:
Avoid Falling into Guilt

Be careful not to assume you must buy into guilt during a Mercury retrograde. It could sneak up on you if you let down your guard. There is a greater potential to be susceptible to guilt during some Mercury retrogrades. You may lose sight of your boundaries and feel too responsible for situations that were not your fault. There might be a particular person who has a way of causing you to feel guilty. Perhaps this person is good at playing the role of the victim. You may be the target of blame for a problem that someone else really caused in the first place.

Mercury retrograde may trigger an old pattern of playing the role of the martyr. Making sacrifices for a worthy cause is a good thing. Serving others is rewarding. This could be part of manifesting your ideals and highest beliefs. Where this selfless theme can get you into trouble is if you are serving the wrong people or groups. This essentially means you don't want to be giving so much of yourself that you lose track of your own goals. The best barometer is to check and see if there is an equal give and take in what or whom you are giving your time and energy to. There may be an underlying feeling of guilt, as though you must make yourself repay others even when it is not necessary. Be on guard for this if you are prone to this type of behavior during a Mercury retrograde.

So how do you convince yourself to avoid guilt during a Mercury retrograde three-week period of time? For one thing, you may need to steer clear of those who know how to manipulate you into agreeing that you created their problems, or at least tell someone you are not going to play their game. Passive-aggressive individuals often will leave you alone if you don't add fuel to the fire. The more you argue with them, the more you make yourself available to be talked into guilt.

The closer you are to someone in a relationship, the more difficult it is to rise above the guilt game. Mercury is a strong communication vehicle. Talking works when you are negotiating with reasonable people. But if you are talking with someone whose only motive is to make you feel guilty to get what they want, then you may have to pull back. Being assertive is a good thing, but wasting your energy and getting no results will leave you confused and frustrated.

If you get some space from people and situations that are pulling you into guilt, this is showing true wisdom. Mercury can provide you with great insight if you distance yourself from those who might be causing you to feel overly obligated to fix their lives. When you have equality in a partnership, the other person does not always want you to save them from a problem. Guilt will cause you to lose your perspective. Saving someone over and over from taking responsibility for their life gets tiring. Your relationship will lack the balance it needs. Mercury retrograde cycles sometimes bring out a tendency to rescue others. Your awareness to begin recognizing this pattern will empower you. Your communication will be clearer. Your relationships will be much more enjoyable.

Tip 20 for Surviving Mercury Retrograde: Unfreeze Your Creative Energy

Don't try to change the world in one day. Remember that your creative energy may sense a dramatic shift at the beginning of a Mercury retrograde. Your schedule or a project may seem like a tall mountain to climb. Mercury has a lot of detail sensibility to offer your mind. Taking one slow step at a time is fine. As a matter of fact, the first step can be the hardest. Thinking about how difficult a goal is to accomplish can discourage you from getting started. Putting an idea into motion may be all of the momentum you require. Breaking a large goal down into smaller bits is a way to keep your mind from worrying about getting finished. Have you heard of the "Swiss Cheese Theory"? This is systematically punching holes in a complex problem. This is a method to get your creativity to thaw out.

It might help to start with a part of a plan that you perceive as the easiest, just to get yourself going. Your mind will get into step with a retrograde cycle when it sees you have a sense of direction. If you have ways to relax your mind, it could help as well. Getting centered through meditation may help you. If you are a high-energy type of person, then some physical exercise could unlock your creative thinking.

Knowing you will get a reward for each step you take in getting your plan done is another way to inspire you. It doesn't have to be a major gift to you. Just knowing there is a payoff for each step of forward progress you make may open the door to expressing your creative power.

Sometimes during a Mercury retrograde your mind really is waiting for you to put it into motion. Think of yourself as the director of the show and your mind as the lead actor. You have to send your mind the right cues to get it to follow your direction. This explanation may sound too simple, but believe it or not, there are times, especially during Mercury's retrograde dance with us, when it only takes pointing your mind at what you need to get done to get your creativity moving. Your mind will often need an extra prompt during this three-week time period. Don't take it personally, because everybody else is likely needing to do the same thing. Your creative energy will flow more smoothly when your mind is pointed at a target. It does not need to be complicated. Remember that you are only trying to get into first gear to get a process activated.

Tip 21 for Surviving Mercury Retrograde: Don't Hide Behind Your Intellect

Mercury offers a wonderful variety of ways to communicate your ideas and get them across to others clearly. During its three week-retrograde excursion, there could be an extra temptation to hide behind your intellect. This will not get you in trouble in impersonal dealings like in the business world. Exchanging information with work colleagues is expected to be a bit more formal. Trying to get a lower price from a salesperson on something you want to buy requires you to wear your business hat. The retrograde might actually help you decipher better ways to negotiate what you need to get from others.

There is a fine line between the mental and emotional worlds during a Mercury retrograde. But to your mind it may seem like there is a firewall between both regions. The intellect can grow quite strong during a Mercury retrograde. The challenge is to successfully cross back and forth to respond appropriately to the situations you encounter.

When you are talking to a lover or family member and you are wearing an intellectual mask to conceal your feelings, it will distance you greatly from them. People are not going to feel they can trust you if you are not being honest about your emotions. You don't want to get trapped into thinking you can only communicate on an intellectual level if a situation is asking more from you on the emotional level. Mercury retrograde sometimes will put you into a strong mental framework that will require you to make an extra effort to switch gears from the impersonal to the personal. You may not even realize you are falling out of touch with expressing an emotion. If someone who knows you on the deepest of levels is asking you to talk more openly about how you feel about a situation,

you may need to push yourself to do so. You might be surprised to find that it is not that hard to be more honest about
your true feelings once you start talking. It is like priming the
emotional pump. Balancing your mental and your emotional
expression leads to greater harmony during a Mercury retrograde. You will be happier and your closest people connections will be there for you when you need them the most.

Tip 22 for Surviving Mercury Retrograde: Balance Your Work and Leisure Time

Mercury retrograde presents an opportunity to balance work
and play in your life. There could be a tendency during certain
Mercury retrogrades to forget to rest. The worry about finishing a project by a deadline is a driving force. It could find you
pushing yourself to the extreme. There are times when all of
us need to go beyond the call of duty because of a situation
that requires it. Just be careful you are not working more than
you need to. If you ignore the people closest to you, it will
cause tension with them.

You may find that your work increases in production if
you spend some quality time with a lover or friend. A vacation away from work actually can empower your work world.
Balancing work and play is great wisdom. There is a part of
the brain that needs a break from work, especially if you are
on overload. So remember that you are not wasting time
when looking to relax. It increases your productivity in the
long run.

Hiding in your work to avoid dealing with a problem could
occur during a Mercury retrograde. This is another reason

that your work life could get out of alignment with your leisure time. Be sure you are not making a situation worse by not dealing with it. Work offers a nice way to escape from facing an obstacle. There are times when going to a job is therapeutic because at least you can see the results of your actions. This is a positive thing in your life. Maybe you need some time to think about how you will handle a problem. But if you are running away from facing adversity, it will only cause problems to escalate. Don't lose sight of the fact that spending time with people and even pets who care about you makes life more fun.

Tip 23 for Surviving Mercury Retrograde:
Use Pink Noise

Pink noise is the universe's way of giving us sound that helps us find the midpoint between order and disorder. Think of it as sound waves that put you in the eye of the hurricane, where the storm is the calmest. If you are naturally a meditative type who easily drifts into tranquil states, you may not require any background sounds to quiet your mind. But if you are a person who tends to be nervous or can't sit still easily, then meditation might not work as well for you. Pink noise simply means having some type of repetitive, pleasing sound present while you are alone in your home or office. It could be soft music, a CD with calming nature sounds, or some other sound that has a centering effect. Sound waves have the capacity to keep you calm and even energized. Another perk is that your sleep may even deepen.

Mercury stimulates our mind to think and to be curious. This is a good thing. A Mercury retrograde can ramp up our thought processes to a faster speed. A retrograde does not always produce a slowing-down effect. So if a quiet home or work space seems to make you nervous, then having some relaxing noise present may relax your nervous system. You might need to experiment a little and see what type of sound you require.

It is even possible that just having a television show you like on in the background, even if you are not focusing on it, will have a positive influence on your nervous system. The same formula won't work for each of us, not even during every Mercury retrograde. You will need to customize which type of sound will work well for you. The barometer will be if you feel more centered and productive. Perhaps it is sensing that you are not alone that has a comforting and reassuring quality.

The main point about pink noise is the rich, tranquilizing tone it offers your inner being. This could be just what you need to help you get better mileage from your ideas during a Mercury retrograde.

Tip 24 for Surviving Mercury Retrograde: Lead with Your Intuition

Leading with your intuition may not be easy, but it could be the way to break through a mental block during a Mercury retrograde. So how do you do this? There is no easy, one-size-fits-all solution for every situation. You may surprise yourself if you slow down in the midst of a puzzling dilemma. The answer to your own question could be at your fingertips. Mercury retrograde energy is trying to guide you past—or maybe it is better to say around—your conscious mind. The conscious mind is always filtering out information for us. Sometimes it acts as a filter to keep out information we don't need and that might not be in our best interest. The trick is not letting your mind treat your intuition as though it is an unwanted intruder and not something useful.

I said in my book *Intuition and Your Sun Sign* that a certain degree of mental toughness is needed to connect with your intuition. This is very true. If you stay determined to see a project through to the end, your intuition will manifest if you believe in it. It is not an esoteric process reserved for certain people. We all have intuition. Your conscious mind, which helps you remain logical and grounded, is vital to your success. Together with your intuitive nature, the two can help you perceive clearly. Occasionally each of us has to find a technique or method to get out of the way and let our intuition come forward. It may be taking a meditation break or in the midst of a walk that an intuitive breakthrough suddenly occurs. It may be while you are trying to think your way through a problem that your intuition will push your mind out of the way.

If you simply acknowledge you have intuition, this will go a long way in making it part of your everyday life. It can become part of your problem-solving process on a regular basis. It starts to happen instinctively the more you believe in your intuition. It takes practice to keep this part of you vibrant. Then, when a Mercury retrograde comes along, it does make it easier to flow with the retrograde process. The experience will not seem as foreign. Your intuition can assist you in surviving and perceiving accurately the messages of a Mercury retrograde cycle. There is a payoff in using your intuition. It relieves the apprehension you may be caught up in during a Mercury retrograde. Intuition recharges your mental energy in a very special way and can help you navigate through this retrograde period more confidently.

Intuition acts as a firewall against negative thinking. It keeps you vigilant to put your best optimistic foot forward. It gives you the strength to persevere through all types of situations.

Tip 25 for Surviving Mercury Retrograde: Tweak Your Short-Range Plans

It isn't necessary to rethink your major life goals during a Mercury retrograde. It isn't like your life gets completely turned upside down during every Mercury retrograde. After all, Mercury makes this movement in the sky three or four times a year, so you don't want to overreact to this cycle each time it occurs. As a matter of fact, it is not a good idea to completely rearrange your priorities this often. But a slight tweak to what you see as your short-term future goals may keep you motivated. You might rewrite some of your script during the retrograde cycle of Mercury. You may be glad later that you believed in this new insight that may seem like it snuck into your mind from out of nowhere. It could be that a new idea will need to be kept on the back burner and turn out to be useful when you need it later at the right time and place.

Mercury retrograde has an unorthodox way of shaking loose hidden material in our mind. Scientists have said we use very little of the information available to us tucked away in the recesses of our brain. Maybe they are right. But then again, you don't necessarily need all of these volumes of material all at once. But every once in a while during a Mercury retrograde, you might find yourself spontaneously rethinking an important plan. You may perceive an easier path to making a dream come true.

Mercury Turning Direct: The Jet Lag Following the Mercury Retrograde

Immediately you might feel a sense of relief when Mercury ends its three-week retrograde period. Your internal clock starts to get in tune again with the external world. Life may seem good again. It's easier to move forward with your plans. Your thoughts and feet are marching together again rather than being in conflict. Give yourself a well-deserved pat on the back for making your way through another Mercury retrograde.

You might be able to look back at the Mercury retrograde with an appreciation for what you did gain insight into. Because of the processing intensity produced by a Mercury retrograde, it may take a little time to feel like you have landed fully in the present again. In the first few days of this Mercury direct time period, you could still be experiencing mental fatigue and not thinking quite as sharp. There is often a feeling of jet lag when Mercury initially turns direct. It is as though our mental faculties are making a readjustment to this change of direction. Don't worry if this occurs. Sometimes it is a slow process. The rest of the world is making the same transition, whether they realize it or not. Remember that all of the people on the planet are undergoing the same thing, so you are not alone. Their faces may not reveal it, but some of their actions for sure will. Be patient with those people you are close to. This includes individuals you work with at the same job. Remember that they too are making a similar adjustment to Mercury moving direct again.

Take your time and know you will be thinking and moving again at normal speed shortly after Mercury makes its move to direct. It takes a large ship a considerable amount of time to make a U-turn. It takes the earth itself twenty-four hours to turn on its axis. We often forget this. So it may take your mind a few days to turn around and move forward.

If you go on with your life, your thinking will bounce back to the way in which you are accustomed before you know it. The stimulating energy of Mercury will arouse your best mental energy quickly. The less you look back at what you may have had to endure during the Mercury retrograde, the better off you will be.

The first day or two following a Mercury retrograde may find you getting tired faster than usual. It is the energy shift from retrograde to direct that is causing this to happen. This is similar to the switch from daylight saving time to standard time, or vice versa. When you take a long plane trip to a different time zone, after you land there is a jet lag. You feel more tired than usual. Your mind and body need to adjust. The same thing happens when Mercury makes a direction change. The mind and body need time to move according to the change in Mercury's motion.

You won't respond the same way every time following a Mercury retrograde. There could be occasions when you hit the ground running as soon as Mercury turns direct. Your entire being is ready to launch forward with a sense of being on a mission. Then again, there may be those Mercury retrograde time periods when made your mind, body, and spirit do a backward flip. These are the Mercury retrogrades that will challenge you to find the inner strength and willpower to proceed full speed ahead once again.

Correcting Missteps During a Mercury Retrograde

There will be times during a Mercury retrograde when you realize you have made a mistake. This could be while working on a project. It is inevitable that doing some things over again is going to be necessary while you are dealing with this retrograde time period. Don't get too upset by this. It may be that you will perceive a better way of doing something that will require less time and money. The efficiency quality of Mercury might show you a shortcut to getting something accomplished. This is very much par for the course. Editing a plan or job might improve what you set out to do in the first place. If you find yourself overthinking how to correct a mistake, take a break and let your mind get centered. The interesting thing about a Mercury retrograde is that it will show you the way to fix a mistake if you don't get too frantic. The more nervous you get, the more difficult it will be to find your way out of a problem. There is a tendency to get too bombarded by outside stimuli. You may even have to distract yourself by doing something fun or anything that takes your mind off your worry. It is better to analyze the situation when you are clear-headed.

Is there a chance that you wish you had not said something to someone during a Mercury retrograde? If this occurs, you have a decision to contemplate. If you think you are going to make matters worse by trying to fix what you communicated the wrong way, then if at all possible it might be wiser to wait until Mercury goes direct. If you cannot wait that long to interact with the person once again, just make sure you feel mentally calm and clear before trying it again.

The good thing about this particular planetary retrograde is that it does have that extra-special capacity to allow you to see a better way to get a message across to someone without causing too much fallout. If there is a good possibility that you might be too critical of a person, you would be wise to think this through clearly. If you think someone will attack you with more criticism than you want to endure, then it might be a good idea to let the situation cool down. Try to see both sides of an issue. You don't want to escalate a problem with a person. Mercury is a great planet to influence you to be more objective when it is working favorably for you. You can't really control what someone else might say to you if their feelings are very hurt. Time may be the best healer. So try to use good, clear judgment in approaching someone once again about a touchy subject.

Sometimes timing means everything. You may have promised more than you could really do for someone. This would be a good time to backtrack and more realistically offer what is possible for you to do for them. Biting off more than you can chew, as the old saying goes, does occur from time to time during a Mercury retrograde. Think in terms of a win-win agreement with the other person to get the best results and lessen the tension. This could involve making a verbal agreement with a company for some work you want to do for them. Maybe you did not understand how much of your time would be taken up by a job. It would be good to level with the place of business to make sure your expectations stay on the same page.

The important thing to remember is that missteps can be fixed. Mercury retrograde can make your head spin out of control. Knowing how to get back to your mental center is crucial in making sound and accurate decisions. Your choices gain power through maintaining a positive attitude. The old saying that "this too shall pass" may have been written to help all of us get through a Mercury retrograde. What might look like a bad choice you made can be corrected. The key is taking your time to consider all of your options.

Positive and Negative Ways to Experience a Mercury Retrograde	
Positive Expression	*Negative Expression*
Attention to detail	Shortsightedness
Positive outlook	Negative thinking
Reasonable expectations	Obsessed with perfection
Creative imagination	Stuck in the box
Good insights	Being overly critical
Adaptability	Inflexibility

This chart is a reminder about some of the most challenging themes of a Mercury retrograde. Remember that anything frustrating you during these three retrograde weeks can be converted into a more positive experience.

Mercury retrograde offers extra intensity to pay attention to details. It is always a good idea to make sure you are taking a second look to make sure you have not overlooked something important that is essential to completing a job. Editing an idea or project is often easier to do during a Mercury retrograde. The thing you need to watch out for is becoming too shortsighted and not seeing the big picture. If you find yourself obsessing over little details, it might keep you from finishing what you set out to accomplish. You will find greater joy and harmony when you don't allow yourself to get lost in worry about the outcome of situations.

Maintaining a positive attitude makes for a much better Mercury retrograde experience. Your creative flow may not miss a beat if you see the cup as at least half full. Your mental and physical health get a big boost when you navigate around gloomy perspectives. Negativity weighs down your opportunities for success. The joy you seek has a much better chance to occur when you walk to a positive beat.

Keep your expectations reasonable during a Mercury retrograde. This is the surest method to avoid frustration. If you can only get the initial steps of a project started, that is okay. It is better than forcing things to happen too fast and having to do them over again. Don't go perfection-crazy, or you will find yourself becoming too self-critical and overanalyzing others. Remember this is only a three-week time period. Be patient. There is a good chance you are doing a lot better than you think. Focus more on what is going right.

Your creative power can flourish during a Mercury retrograde. Believing in your ability is essential for your creative impulses to be released successfully. Allow your intuition to guide you. Have faith in your talents and there is no end to how well things will go. Watch out for too much self-doubt. It will hold you back. If you stay attached to limiting ideas, they won't allow your new energy to manifest. Let your spontaneity have a strong voice.

During a Mercury retrograde, you could have great insights into how best to achieve your own goals and may see a better way for others to get a plan accomplished. Your mental strength might intensify. Your mind could penetrate through obstacles that once seemed impossible. Where you need to exercise some wisdom is in not offering too much unsolicited opinions to other people. It will come off as being overly critical of their ideas. If you show you are listening, your advice will be more well received.

If you can adapt to changing circumstances during a Mercury retrograde, you will enjoy the journey. It is not uncommon for unexpected things to occur during this three-week cycle. If you become too inflexible, you may miss out on an opportunity. Something that presents itself as being too big a risk could be your ticket to abundance. The more you flow with a temporary change in circumstances, the more you will enjoy the Mercury retrograde ride. Experiences that challenge your comfort zone may be chances to stimulate your mind into new thinking.

Mercury Stationary Motion

When a planet like Mercury appears to be standing still when viewed from the earth, it is referred to as being in stationary motion. This motionless appearance occurs when Mercury's orbit is about to reverse its movement either from direct to retrograde (called stationary retrograde) or from retrograde to direct (called stationary direct). In reality, this is an illusion, because a planet does not really change direction or stop moving. It just looks like the planet is doing this mysterious dance. The standing still is known as a planet's *station*. A Mercury station lasts for one day when the planet is about to change direction either from retrograde to direct or from direct to retrograde.

What does this change in planetary motion imply? It is believed by most astrologers that a planet's influence is greatly intensified when it is stationary. A stationary direct planet generally offers you a powerful opportunity to put a planet to work for you. A stationary retrograde planet in many instances can be used successfully but does require more reflection before putting the energy into action for yourself.

When Mercury is about to move from direct to retrograde motion and remaining stationary retrograde for one day, it is a good time to carefully determine if you need to make a decision on this day. Generally speaking, it is likely a wise policy to be as sure as you can about a choice. If you really have no option but to move on a decision during this Mercury stationary retrograde day, just be sure you weighed all of the possibilities carefully. You may be one of those very intuitive individuals who can move with great accuracy on this special retrograde day. Patience is good to utilize to make sure you are not moving out of confusion. Many people find a Mercury stationary retrograde day great for meditation and relaxation. It is a good day to put your worries aside. It is for sure a day to spend time with your favorite people and pastimes. The main message here is to try to stay centered and grounded if you are faced with a key decision.

When Mercury is getting ready to move from retrograde to direct motion and remain stationary direct for a day, you may sense that it is a great time to launch a plan. It can feel like the entire universe is cheering you on to move forward. Your mind and intuition can seem to be magically on the same page. Your entire being rejoices that the three-week Mercury retrograde time period is once again coming to a close. It is time to get on with your life with renewed vigor. You greet the new day with great enthusiasm. If you felt hesitant during the Mercury retrograde, you can now give yourself permission to move spontaneously to pursue your goals.

The Silver Lining Following a Mercury Retrograde

What might be your reward for surviving the mental anguish of a Mercury retrograde? Try thinking of these few weeks as a *mental tune-up*. This may be the first time you have heard Mercury retrograde described this way. The universe is trying to relax your mental intensity and that of everyone else. This does not mean you should stop putting out your best effort. It is saying you may be able to learn more productive ways to express your ideas. Slowing down does not need to be interpreted as stopping. Sometimes in the midst of chaos during a Mercury retrograde you can suddenly see your way out of a jam. What looked like a huge mountain to climb was not so big after all. The stress in your mind could have been making your problems appear bigger than they were.

Quickly after a Mercury retrograde ends, you might be able to appreciate what you have learned. As you process those weeks of the retrograde, your mind can discover new insights. A lot is revealed to us during a Mercury retrograde. Initially this may not be so obvious when Mercury turns direct. It is during the period of time when Mercury first turns direct that we might be able to realize it.

A sense of renewal is possible, or maybe even a rebirth. A mental cleansing sometimes takes place during a Mercury retrograde. Negative energy gets removed, although during the retrograde each of us gets in the habit of not readily giving it up. Our attachment to old thought patterns is strong. This is just part of being human. There is nothing wrong with establishing routines. We all need them to feel grounded and even secure. The beauty of Mercury retrograde is that it is a time to transcend worn-out ideas and trade them in for something new. It is a gift of this mysterious cycle. Hidden in the apparent confusion we may experience during the retrograde might be the answer as to how to rise above an obstacle on our path. This is a true silver lining.

Chapter Three
Venus:
The Relationship Planet

Areas Influenced by Venus: Socializing, romance, stability, partnerships, affluence, self-esteem

Elements Associated with Venus: Earth and air

Signs Ruled by Venus: Taurus and Libra

Venus Retrograde Gifts: Refueled social awareness, new appreciation for abundance

Duration of Venus Retrograde: Six weeks

Before taking a look at Venus when it is in its retrograde cycle, let's consider the manner in which this planet operates when traveling direct. Venus motivates all of us to develop sound partnerships. Venus will entice you to seek a soulmate. Having a reliable companion makes life feel more rewarding. If this does not interest you, Venus will stimulate a drive to find valuable friendships. Having a key ally or two makes for a smoother journey in trying to figure out how to create a meaningful life. Venus does not believe you should be a lone wolf and live in solitude. It is quite the contrary with this relationship giant of the universe. Being in the company of others and pulsating to an inner desire to find likeminded individuals is part of the Venusian world.

Venus is often referred to as the "goddess of love" in Roman mythology. She was associated with beauty, sex, fertility, and prosperity. The ancient Greeks called her Aphrodite, in regard to love and sexuality. Just as the brightness of Venus in the sky charms you into admiring her beauty, this darling planet of the universe will direct you on how to show love and affection toward others. This love intoxicant will guide you to establish emotional closeness with others.

Enjoying the finer things in life is another attribute of Venus. This includes eating the foods you find tasty, going to movies, dancing, and other forms of entertainment. After all, this is the planet beckoning to you to take the time to indulge in rest and relaxation. If you take this tendency to the extreme, people will accuse you of being lazy, wasting time, and being too self-indulgent. So with some wisdom you will begin to figure out how far to take this pleasure principle. Nobody should criticize you for a well-deserved vacation, right?

Venus in astrology is the ruler of two signs: earthy Taurus and airy Libra. It is the Taurus association that encourages you to find stability. This can take the form of putting down solid roots in a community or having enough money to pay all of your bills. Knowing you have built solid relationships and have everyday life experiences you can count on during rain or sunshine is part of the Venus package. It is the Libra connection to Venus that influences you to find a soulmate.

The Libra expression represents the Venus stimulation in your mind to seek a peer group that reflects your values and your need for a social life. The innate drive to share your life with a special someone comes right out of this side of Venus. Both dimensions of Venus are keys to finding happiness.

If you prefer to reserve the right to make a major commitment to a person until later in life or not at all, Venus will not sit in judgment of you. This matchmaker of the sky would rather you take your time and find someone who treats you as an equal. It is balancing your own needs with those of friends, lovers, or family members that is a special message from Venus. You won't be happy if you continually sacrifice your own goals to please others. People won't like it if you demand your own way in all major decisions. Venus will attempt to guide you to the middle ground to strengthen your partnerships.

Negotiating business deals is yet another gift from this even-tempered planet who glides peacefully perched high above us. The hope from this heavenly wanderer is that we will find some peace of mind in living our daily lives. Making choices can be a source of tension. Expressing your needs to get a raise in salary or to get a lover to hear what you really need from them takes courage. Venus will whisper to you from time to time that life is a series of negotiations. You won't always get your demands met. But then again, you do have the right to make it known what you need in order to be happy.

Weighing options comes under the rulership of Venus. The key is being able to make a decision. Sometimes both choices that are staring you in the eyes look good. It might be painful to finally make a selection. The liberation in moving forward can feel refreshing. Peace is restored. Life stabilizes until the next big decision awaits you.

Possessions are another Venus theme. What do you need to own in order to find personal satisfaction? This is an important question as Venus awakens your drive for success. There is personal power in ownership, but there can be an illusionary trap in wealth as well. Does acquiring more wealth free you to create more options and open more doors for you and those you care about? If the answer is yes, it will be exciting and energizing to buy what the world has to offer. If collecting things and living only to get richer starts to stunt your growth, it might result in unhappiness. The trick is not to let your ambition and wealth throw your life out of balance.

You more than likely have heard the saying that "life is not always fair." Venus would quickly interject with a mediating tone to "find the fairness." That is Venus-speak. When dealing with others, look for the higher ground. Try to walk in someone else's shoes, even if they don't look like a good fit, just to get a different perspective. Be objective. Stay calm when someone is trying to provoke you. Why? So you can see the best way to lessen the tension. Venus would not tell you to be a doormat. You can defend your position. But when you become a listener, you can fight from a true position of strength. There is a better-than-average potential to get a positive outcome. There could be a win-win result if you and an adversary stay levelheaded. Venus is inherently a peacemaker, but not a foolish one. The idea is to encourage a compromise that you and someone else can tolerate.

There is a job and career dimension to Venus that emanates from its Taurus roots. Finding a work situation that comes close to matching your values is a way of aligning yourself with Venus. This is basically what this good-natured planet is all about. If your job isn't what you had hoped to find, then at least working with people you respect and enjoy is another way to be content. The Libra dimension of Venus will encourage you to be part of a team of people you like to work among. If you are a work-alone type, then the work itself becomes that much more important in terms of its need to inspire you. Whatever your work circumstances, getting paid enough to make you feel valuable might be a deciding factor in keeping you in a profession. The main Venus concern here is that you feel justly rewarded in either the salary, recognition and being compensated for the level of stress you are facing. Giving yourself the chance to find a new opportunity could be the way to happiness.

Even cultivating a hobby can be a way to connect with Venus. Finding things to do that keep your mind active can be part of a Venus expression. This comes under the Venus department of entertaining your mind. Whether you get into gardening, cooking, playing music, exercising, or taking educational classes, Venus is there to cheer you on to a journey of self-discovery.

Your Sun Sign, Your Sign Element, and Venus Retrograde: A Dynamic Triad

In the previous Mercury chapter, it was shown how your Sun sign, being a member of one of the four elements found in nature, will find you responding to a planet's retrograde time period in a particular way. Your Sun sign is a powerful influence in your life. It is connected to one of the four elements: fire, earth, air and water. Because your Sun sign belongs to one of the four elements, you will interact with a Venus retrograde cycle in a unique manner. You will not react to each Venus retrograde time period in the same way.

The element discussions that follow are meant to serve as a guide to help you tune in to a Venus retrograde time period. This combination of your Sun sign and its corresponding element join together with a Venus retrograde to offer you new ways to relate to the world around you. The three join forces to help you clarify choices that best reflect your values and point the way to personal empowerment. Your relationship tendencies could grow more reflective under a Venus retrograde. You could be rethinking what you need from others to improve a partnership. It could be that you will look for ways to resolve an old issue with a person.

In reality, each of us is a mixture of the four elements. They are part of our psychological nature and self-expression. Your Sun sign is a major player in your creative self-expression and showing the world your ability. If you are new to astrology, you know a lot about yourself in terms of your own element even if you don't realize it. Knowing your Sun sign element helps you tune in to the messages of a Venus retrograde time period. This will give you a peek into how to adjust and survive harmoniously with Venus retrograde. What follows are brief descriptions of how your Sun sign and element interact with a Venus retrograde.

Venus: The Relationship Planet   83

The Fire Signs (Aries, Leo, Sagittarius) and Venus Retrograde

If your Sun sign is a member of the fire element, your usual carefree way of interacting with others could take on a more thoughtful tone during a Venus retrograde. Actually this may become apparent right at the beginning of the cycle. Don't let this upset you. A fiery person like you may be accustomed to dealing directly with others. What is interesting during a Venus retrograde is that you might be feeling like you want to get right to the point with someone but it is the other person who is acting like they want to deal with the situation at a later time. The key is not to get frustrated with delays in getting results. You may find that going slower will yield better solutions to problems. Your reaction time to responding to the demands of others may go into a slowdown. Why does this occur? More than likely it is because you want to weigh your options more carefully than you usually do. When Venus turns direct again, you will be that much more prepared to act with decisiveness.

Your business decisions may require greater contemplation. Often this will be due to situations beyond your control. Think of it as testing your patience. Sometimes it could even feel like your willpower is being challenged more than usual by others. You might run into a snag closing out a deal, requiring you to put your problem-solving hat on. The fire element drives you to get a fast fix to a problem. A retrograde Venus is a bit of a contradiction to your normal way of operating on the business level, but this does not mean that you can't bring a plan to fruition with some determination.

If your Sun sign is fiery Aries (March 20–April 19), your natural inclination to interact spontaneously with others could be a bit slower than you are accustomed to during a Venus retrograde. Your push to defend a position could seem more restrained. The universe may be asking you to take your time and evaluate your need to accelerate into a new direction more carefully. In the long run, moving slower in forming new partnerships may be in your best interest. Taking extra time to think through a negotiating strategy for a business deal or a salary increase may prove wise. Revisiting a solution to an old problem might test your patience but be liberating at the same time. Being in the company of supportive friends is a stabilizing influence.

If your Sun sign is fiery Leo (July 22–August 22), your forceful tendency to get others to notice you may not be as strong during a Venus retrograde, or it could seem like people are not responding to your needs as quickly as you like. Making situations bend to your willpower may meet with more resistance than usual. Don't take this personally. That lion-like roar you are known for is still within you. The Venus retrograde forces at work slow down your immediate reaction to conquer a challenge. The important thing to remember is not to panic. You are just as able to rise above a problem as you usually are. It is just that this retrograde time period is asking you to study your options with greater scrutiny. Your creative power is just as intense, even though it may appear on the surface to have lost a beat in its rhythm. With that Leo tenacity of yours, there is no new life direction to fear. Your highest ideals and most cherished goals can still be achieved. You can maintain stability by paying attention to those you love while moving briskly toward your goals.

If your Sun sign is fiery Sagittarius (November 21–December 21), your customary way of motivating yourself may seem more sluggish. It could seem like the world is slower to encourage your dreams to be a success. Don't let this bother you. It may be that you need to get more focused on your goals. It does not mean that each day during a Venus retrograde you won't get the support you require to pursue a goal. It is only saying it could be a great time to make sure what you hope to accomplish is in alignment with your values. Your partnerships could deepen in commitment during this cycle. It could be a time when a current relationship will find renewal. Relationships that no longer meet your needs may be reevaluated. Rewarding yourself as well as those you care about is a stabilizing force.

The Air Signs (Gemini, Libra, Aquarius) and Venus Retrograde

If your Sun sign is a member of the air element, your nervous system could get overstimulated in your social interactions during a Venus retrograde, probably because you can't process the information coming at you from others as fast as usual. This does not mean you should not be as socially engaging in your normal way, but only that you could get tired more easily from over-extending your time with people. Your perceptions about certain individuals could deepen. Your expectations of what you want from others may change, and what they hope to receive from you could go through some changes as well. You might need to consider whether your job and professional aspirations are meeting your needs. A goal may need to be tweaked to ensure positive results. A plan for the future might go at a slower pace. But be ready for everything to move much faster in forward motion when Venus moves direct once again.

If your Sun sign is airy Gemini (May 20–June 20), a Venus retrograde could interfere somewhat with your usual way of socially interacting with others. Communication with those closest to you may be more challenging. Each of you could feel like you are reading out of opposite playbooks. It will require greater patience and understanding to reach mutually agreeable perspectives about life. Your business ideas may flourish in your head but be harder to get across to those you want to impress during this retrograde time period. It does not mean you can't move a plan forward now. You may need to find a more clever method to make your business insights clearer to others. Think in terms of using the right hook to bring in someone you really are trying to reel in to your way of thinking. This is a good cycle to plan a winning strategy even if you do have to wait for the Venus retrograde to end and ride the powerful promising waves of this planet's direct movement.

If your Sun sign is airy Libra (September 22–October 22), your desire to impress others with your social savvy may not feel as vibrant under a Venus retrograde. This is not saying your diplomatic skills will be lessened. People could appear more distant or detached. It is possible that this is their perception of you. So don't be surprised if your wanting more closeness from a friend or lover is not readily embraced. It might have more to do with people being distracted by their own goals for a better tomorrow. Your business ideas and plans for entertainment need to be carefully gone over. The retrograde Venus might prove to be a test in getting the world to cooperate with your time schedule. A serious strategy can be prepared during Venus retrograde and forcefully launched when this planet moves direct in motion.

If your Sun sign is Airy Aquarius (January 20–February 19), your usual method of displaying your spontaneous social instincts could get disrupted by Venus retrograde. This cycle may find you acting with greater caution. It may be that people you already know and those new individuals you encounter are acting in ways that seem foreign to you. This does not mean you will be feeling this way during the entire Venus retrograde. Just don't be surprised if you find that you need to watch how you communicate more carefully. Your words may be upsetting to someone even though you did not intend for this to occur. People may offend you more easily than normal. So it may be that carefully thinking through a response to someone will prove wiser in the long run. Your business plans and job goals will likely meet with some degree of delay during this cycle. It is possible that what seems like an obstacle could be converted into a winning formula. Your most serious ambitions may find an open door that becomes visible when Venus moves direct in motion.

The Earth Signs (Taurus, Virgo, Capricorn) and Venus Retrograde

If your Sun sign is a member of the earth element, a Venus retrograde experience can send your linear way of defining your boundaries with others into a reflective mode. You may not be as clear how much closeness or distance you want from people. Don't worry. This does not mean you will feel this way for the entire six weeks of a Venus retrograde time period. It could be that a friend or partner is displaying this behavior more than you on a day-to-day basis. It might require clearer communication to maintain clarity in relationships. Schedules regarding work can become more disruptive. You likely will need to be more flexible to avoid getting frustrated. Your determination to finish a project can be just as strong. It is very possible that combining work and pleasure will actually help you get more done in a shorter amount of time during a Venus retrograde. Remember that Venus is trying to show you that having some fun and leisure time is a good thing, so making time in your schedule for a vacation or a favorite pastime is wonderful wisdom to utilize during a Venus retrograde. Your concentration will be better if you take breaks during the workday to rest your mind.

If your Sun sign is earthy Taurus (April 19–May 20), a Venus retrograde could dampen your enthusiasm to take a risk. But since you are one of the signs that Venus rules, there is the possibility that even during a retrograde you can dare yourself into taking a chance on a new opportunity. As a Taurus, you are likely perceived as being cautious with your money and investments. A retrograde Venus could have you wanting to be extra careful when making new purchases. It is wise for you to look around during this cycle to make sure you are getting the best deal. You might be reluctant to be as socially outgoing as usual. A desire for more private time may be your way of refueling your mind, body, and spirit. You could feel more secure being in the company of people to whom you are the closest. This retrograde time period does not have to be uneventful, but some extra planning will keep you from wasting your time and resources. Putting together a career strategy or making plans to take on a major undertaking are good uses of your time during a Venus retrograde. When Venus turns direct, you can be ready to fully implement the new ambition.

If your Sun sign is earthy Virgo (August 22–September 22), a Venus retrograde could influence you to reexamine what you think you need from others. It is just as true that people might be wanting more from you. You probably will be wanting to know if the give and take is equal. A commitment in a relationship may deepen. Then again, you could be questioning the need for a particular friendship. In your work world, it is highly possible that you will want more from a job. Patience is important to make sure you are not leaving a good opportunity for something that is risky. Your determination to put excellence into a project can intensify during a Venus retrograde. Be reasonable in what you expect from the result of your actions. Maintaining a positive attitude is vital to your success. Excessive worry needs to be avoided. You will find it much easier to get positive responses to your creative endeavors when Venus once again resumes direct motion.

If your Sun sign is earthy Capricorn (December 21–January 20), a Venus retrograde could find you being extra cautious in terms of your ambitious goals. Slowing down does not necessarily mean you have to stop your forward motion. Your focusing power actually gains intensity with some extra planning. Your negotiating skills might seem less effective during this cycle at first glance. But don't let this fool you. When you make a determined effort, success can still be possible. The important people in your life could perceive you as being extra reserved during this cycle. It might be that you need more time to process the requests from others being made of you. People may seem more demanding than usual. If you don't grow overly anxious in forcing issues with others, life will be more harmonious. It may be more challenging than usual to define relationships clearly. There is a possibility you are trying to figure out what you really value in a partnership during this retrograde cycle. Patience with yourself and others is a key to mutual harmony. Your life will get back on track on all fronts when Venus moves direct once again.

The Water Signs (Cancer, Scorpio, Pisces) and Venus Retrograde

If your Sun sign is a member of the water element, your social instincts could feel like they have gone into freeze mode during a Venus retrograde. It's not that you can't handle your human relations adequately when push comes to shove, but only that you might not be sensing that your spontaneity is there as readily as you like it. A desire for privacy will likely increase. This may not be a bad thing. You may find it easier to focus when you are alone, especially on making major decisions. You might perceive that people don't seem as willing to compromise, and don't be surprised if you are feeling the same way. This may be due to needing more time to come to a decision. Choices are more aggravating to make during a Venus retrograde. It is as though the universe is testing you and everyone else to carefully consider the consequences of a decision before taking action. Even conducting business on a day-to-day basis is not as flowing during a Venus retrograde cycle. You can function in your job as successfully as usual. Just be sure not to let frustration be the motivating force to make a bad decision when a little patience could add clarity to your thinking and produce a more positive outcome. When Venus moves direct, your relationships and negotiating ability will have a more vibrant quality.

If your Sun sign is watery Cancer (June 20–July 22), a Venus retrograde could find you longing for the past in thinking it was better than your present circumstances. Don't let this bother you. Some divine discontent could surface, causing you to view your present circumstances as less rewarding than you think they should be. It might be a wake-up call to reward yourself more. Perhaps you need to create new stimulating experiences. A tendency to pull away from people can be a temporary response to a Venus retrograde. The interesting thing is that during a Venus retrograde, you may tire of time alone and want to burst into the social scene. Making your home a relaxing retreat may soothe your nerves. Your creative energy may be less predictable during this retrograde. Balancing work and relaxation will help you maximize your productivity and give you peace of mind. When Venus turns direct, life will get back to the pace you enjoy.

If your Sun sign is Scorpio (October 22–November 21), a Venus retrograde could find you more reflective than usual about your relationships. Processing past communication exchanges with others could take on a new meaning. What you value in a special someone or your friends could take on a new significance. Wanting to be more appreciated for what you do for others may intensify in importance. Your self-esteem could become empowered in surprising ways during this cycle. A bond with a person may deepen. Some relationships may not seem as important to you at this time. You might scrutinize your work and career needs very carefully. Your search for a new job opportunity might increase. Planning a strategy to enhance your chances for a more abundant life can be on your mind. When Venus moves direct, you may feel it is time to move toward a more promising future in terms of employment and possibly even love.

If your Sun sign is Pisces (February 19–March 20), a Venus retrograde could find you stepping back from your relationships with others to get a more objective view. This does not mean that anything is wrong. A more serious tone may temper your idealism. Stating clearly what you expect from someone helps to keep your boundaries solid. Knowing when you are giving away too much of your time and resources to others is a key component to happiness during a Venus retrograde. Balancing the give and take will tend to stabilize your partnerships during this cycle. Your business and job pursuits may require you to be honest with yourself. Knowing you have enough money to buy what you need might increase in importance during a Venus retrograde. Be sure not to make purchases and overextend your generosity at this time. When Venus turns direct, you will be equipped with clearer thinking on how to proceed in all matters of the heart and business.

Surviving a Venus Retrograde Through Refueling Your Social Instincts and Self-Worth

Retrograde Venus Survival Toolbox

- Maintain your self-esteem.
- Create equality in your partnerships.
- Balance stability and emotional intensity.
- Embrace abundance.
- Believe in a hopeful future.

Venus goes retrograde about every eighteen months. A retrograde Venus excursion lasts for about six weeks. How might this retrograde period influence you? One way this could work, no matter what your Sun sign may be, is that you might be reexamining your relationships and what you hope to expect from them. There is the possibility of feeling more anxious about them and not as sure about your perceptions of others. But then again, you could be pleasantly surprised to find your thinking about a person much clearer. This is the mystery and intriguing impact of a Venus retrograde cycle.

When you read the following Venus retrograde survival tips, consider them a guide to help you better navigate your way through the pitfalls that you may encounter during this cycle of time. Try to envision this as your opportunity to put the messages of Venus into creative opportunities for yourself.

The reason for offering the survival tips is to give you the inside scoop as to what might be going on in your life during a Venus retrograde. These six weeks need not be a source of aggravation. Your relationships can be filled with harmony and peace. Your self-esteem need not drop in altitude or attitude. What you value in life does not need to be compromised. Remember that you are not alone in dealing with a Venus retrograde when it occurs. The whole world is undergoing the same process. You can be more self-assured to deal with whatever comes your way with less fear of the future by utilizing the survival tips.

Tips for Surviving Venus Retrograde

Tip 1 for Surviving Venus Retrograde:
Embrace Your Decisions

Venus retrograde can test the limits of your decisiveness. Putting off decisions can be a painful experience. Weighing your options thoughtfully is a good thing, but constantly swinging back and forth endlessly in your mind is aggravating. You lose time and energy when you torture yourself wondering which choice is the right one. You don't want to get carried away with this during the entire six weeks that Venus is in retrograde motion. Venus, being a fair-minded planet, will sometimes appear to be sending you mixed messages when considering alternatives. It is no accident that Venus does rule the astrological sign of Libra, which has a set of scales as a symbol. Balancing this measuring device to keep your mind and emotions in check takes practice. Deciding between more than one possibility can be hard on your nervous system. In the back of your mind may be that aggravating question of "am I making the right choice?" The energy of Venus, especially in its retrograde movement, awakens you to be very aware of opposites. This can filter down to trying to make up your mind between what looks like two tempting paths to take. It does not always mean that one choice is completely better than another. It could come down to trusting your own instincts. Whatever you decide, it is far better to live with your decision than to get in the habit of second-guessing yourself too much.

If you are a person who tends to make impulsive decisions, it might be a good idea to get a second opinion before making a move on a major decision. There will be people who will like your choices, but there will always be those who question your judgment. In the end, be sure to take the path that feels right to you. This is a key ingredient to happiness, because in the end, you are the person who has to live with whatever is finally decided. Also, you will become truly empowered when you believe in your own decision-making ability. This comes from experience and not fearing if you make a mistake. If it turns out you made the wrong choice, you could very well correct this later. Sometimes during a Venus retrograde it is the embarrassment of making a bad choice that is what really bothers us. So remember not to let your pride get in the way. You won't always be able to get everyone to agree that you made the best choice for yourself.

You may not be able to wait for Venus to turn direct before making a decision. There is always the possibility you can make adjustments later. Try to remember that Venus retrograde will trigger an inner voice that says to move with what best serves your hope to achieve harmony. If you don't hear the message, be patient, because sooner or later the clarity will come when your mind is still enough.

Tip 2 for Surviving Venus Retrograde: Reward Yourself

If you are the type of person who thinks of yourself last in dealing with people, then you need to read this section carefully. Maybe cut it out and put on your refrigerator or someplace where you can view it regularly. It is easy to get lost in other people's problems. Or perhaps you feel too responsible for others, or your attitude comes tumbling down quickly when something goes wrong in your home life or at work. A Venus retrograde may intensify this behavior pattern, so have a plan to lift your spirits. What might this survival package include? Do activities that make you feel good. Don't feel guilty about rewarding yourself. It is easy to neglect what you need to be happy when you are too worried or feel guilty.

It might be a combination of things that will elevate your mind to a better place. Perhaps you would enjoy good food, a movie, being with the people you like, a vacation, new cosmetics, new clothes, a new hairstyle, new books, taking classes, new technology, and even good sex. There are no hard-and-fast rules to lift your mood. Be creative when considering ways to move into a more stimulating atmosphere.

A Venus retrograde might ignite a desire to keep a gratitude journal, which in its own way is yet another way to reward yourself. There is a theory that making a short list of what you are grateful for each day could motivate you to participate in experiences that nourish your mind, body, and spirit.

Receiving is difficult when you don't feel deserving of it. Believe it or not, it takes practice. If you are a lot better at giving than receiving, it will take some time to change the pattern. Venus retrograde is actually a wonderful cycle in which to reverse this trend or at least find a better balance. If the people in your life are not good at giving you what you need, then guess what? You need to take control and give what you need to yourself.

What if you are a person who takes too much and gives back too little? Then try doing the giving. Venus retrograde can balance this out as well. This might sound strange, but giving to others during a Venus retrograde can feel like you are giving something to yourself on the emotional level while you are helping other people feel better about themselves. Rewarding others for what they do or just being in your life is still a way of rewarding yourself!

Self-esteem is directly linked to being able to reward yourself, so it is vital to your happiness to let down your guard to receive what life wants to give you. A Venus retrograde has the capacity to break down your resistance to being good to yourself. You only need to be willing to allow this magical process to work on your behalf. Think of this as developing a newfound intention of opening your mind and heart to accepting what life wants you to receive. You will find yourself attracting the positive experiences you are seeking.

Tip 3 for Surviving Venus Retrograde: Deal with Your Relationship Issues

If there is an issue you want to resolve with a person, a Venus retrograde could be just the right time period to do this. It may even seem like the universe put in just the right prescription for you to get this accomplished. It may not be apparent to you at the start of a Venus retrograde, but over the course of this six-week cycle a strategy could develop in your mind to fix a relationship problem with a lover, friend, employee, or family member. Don't be in a hurry to accomplish this task. Moving slower is wise to keep your thoughts fresh. It can take longer to tune in to the correct steps to fix a relationship problem during a Venus retrograde.

Old or recent disputes need not come between you and someone else. There is always the chance that a situation is truly irresolvable. It is wisdom indeed to know the difference between the two. If you are honest with yourself, you can likely decipher which is true. Believe it or not, a Venus retrograde can deepen your awareness to realize whether settling a squabble with a person is worth your time and energy. If this is a self-defeating situation, then it could be time to let it go as a learning experience. This opens the door for a better relationship opportunity in the future. You likely will be more than ready to avoid getting back into the same type of relationship again. Awareness is the key thing a Venus retrograde can give you, but don't be surprised if it takes a week or two or even three into the retrograde for the insight to be awakened to heal a relationship problem.

Venus is the planet that shows us how to see both sides of an issue. To figure out the best solution to a difference of opinion with another person, you first need to be clear about your own position. If you act with clarity, you feel empowered enough to push for what you need to accomplish mediating your differences. It is this personal power that helps you take the high ground in reaching a compromise. Knowing your own insights into the situation creates an objectivity that allows you to stand back far enough to really perceive what someone else needs from you. Finding the midpoint between two points of view belongs in the diplomacy department of Venus. This planet really has no rival in acting as a referee running interference between two opposing factions.

A Venus retrograde has a lot of healing energy within it to bring you and another person closer to agreeing to disagree. This is one way to get past a problem. You don't need to be a doormat, nor does the other party involved. If you are feeling your own power, it usually will either push an adversary away or bring them closer. If you are shooting for equality or a win-win solution to a problem, then the result is likely to be far more favorable for you and the other person. It is when either of you is fighting for your own position that finding a peaceful solution to an issue is difficult to reach. Avoiding extremes is something to bear in mind. In other words, if one or the other of you is totally intolerant of the other's point of view, a compromise is not going to be reached. The idea is not to think of this as winning at all costs but rather to let each other feel some sense of victory.

Anger can be at the root of a relationship issue. The closer you are to a person, the more heated will be the exchanges, even if you are mentally clear about the situation. You have to allow for some fire to be expressed in the exchange so that you are able to clarify what each of you needs from the other. In some ways it is like letting the steam out of a pressure cooker. The Venus calm and harmony may follow when you get what you don't like about each other's perspectives out of the way. The Venus retrograde cycle has the capacity to allow each of you to see more options to resolve a disagreement. It offers you the flexibility to get through a dispute without either of you getting too mentally and emotionally bruised. There will be a lot less fallout from an argument if you express your feelings openly. It might hurt to hear things you don't like, but in the end it makes it easier to move forward with another person. You may even find that making room in the relationship for your voiced differences makes your bond that much stronger.

Tip 4 for Surviving Venus Retrograde: Don't Say Yes When You Mean No

Venus will sometimes prompt you to be overly accommodating to please others. This could happen more frequently during a Venus retrograde, especially if you are prone to being this way. It might be less tension-provoking to go with the flow and too easily follow the lead of others. Always giving in to the wishes of other people can start to wear on your nerves. It takes some practice to get good at saying no when you need to put yourself first. If you never pursue your own goals because you're always putting someone else first, frustration is bound to result. It is not good for your mental and physical well-being to live in a world where you negate your own hopes and wishes.

Venus is very much a relationship planet that pushes you to seek equality in your partnerships. It isn't that you must always get your own way, but it's important to find harmony in your relationships and have mutual respect for one another's needs. There are times when you will have to be assertive even if it feels awkward or uncomfortable. If you upset someone by putting yourself first, the other person will need to learn to accept that this is going to occur from time to time. The balance you need to establish a successful relationship very much depends on this. Sooner or later you will pull away from someone who is too self-oriented.

It is in the best interests of you and the other person to speak more truthfully about what you need to be happy. A Venus retrograde will give you a lot of opportunities to get this right. Think of it as being offered practice sessions to begin a new way of putting your own goals in the spotlight. It will take a lot of regular effort and positive reinforcement to reverse trends that have not worked in your favor. Old patterns don't change easily. If you are greatly in need of paying attention to what you require to be happy, you could feel selfish in beating to your own drum. Don't let this steer you away from putting yourself at the front of the line. It starts to feel good to witness your own goals getting energized by vibrantly pursuing them.

It could be that you want to be loved or accepted by someone so badly that you are willing to be too compromising. You can't make it your duty to always please others. People should not expect you to be willing to respond as though you have no right to disagree with them. Being accepted for who you are is far better than having to pretend to be someone you are not. Wearing a mask that hides your true self keeps you in limiting circumstances. This may even pertain to belonging to a group. Be careful not to sacrifice too much of your own time just to be part of an organization. Being selfless is admirable, but there are limits.

Even regarding your job there may be times when you have to tactfully say that you can only handle so much of the work. You don't mind being a team player, but you need someone to pay attention to the fact that you are doing all you can handle. Remember, Venus can help you master the art of diplomacy. It may be that you have more power than you realize when negotiating with others. This will take some practice if you have not exercised this side of yourself in the past or have done so infrequently. You can carefully assess a work or business situation to see just how far you can take the word "no." When you try this, you will probably like it.

Tip 5 for Surviving Venus Retrograde: Put a New Job Plan into Action

There may be a particular Venus retrograde that inspires you to take a leap of faith and escape from confining life circumstances that are holding you back. Perhaps you are working in a job or business that has not felt like you for quite some time. Don't beat yourself up for waiting to act. Everyone is faced with this scenario at some point in their life. A situation that once promoted growth is no longer serving that purpose.

Since Venus has a connection to personal values and earning a living, it might just occur to you during a Venus retrograde you are revisiting a desire to move on to a new experience. A search for a job can be done under this cycle. Think of a Venus retrograde as an opportunity to do your homework about new employment prospects. Since Venus is a people-oriented planet, you could even discover another work situation through a friend or previous coworker now employed elsewhere. Perhaps the people you are working with no longer make you happy. Are you looking for a freer or more harmonious work atmosphere? These types of questions surface during a Venus retrograde.

Maybe you are ready to start exploring starting a business. Even if you don't launch it under a Venus retrograde, you could begin formulating a strategy to get it off the ground successfully. This is a good time to look into getting a loan for a business, if you need it. If you need equipment or supplies, you can use a Venus retrograde to search for the best deals for the money. It may make it easier for you to stay in your current job if you plant the seeds for a side profession with the hope of doing it full-time one day. It often takes time to build a new business into a solid entity. Having this other plan in motion could give you the patience to stay longer at a current job. The stimulation of your other work aspiration could make it easier to maintain your stamina to stay at your present job until the time is right to leave, or just going on interviews with other employers could provide you with the same type of willingness to stay put for the time being. Venus will remind you to think in terms of stability and keeping your eyes open for the type of creative expression that makes a strong statement about your ability.

There is another key concern when looking for another job: earning more money. You might know you are worth a lot more than you are now receiving from an employer. A Venus retrograde may not open the door for a new start, but it might remind you not to give up on keeping hope alive. If you maintain a positive outlook, you have a greater chance of attracting more abundance. Don't ever sell yourself short. There might be some skills you possess that you need to value more and that, through emphasizing them, could land you a new job. Sometimes an employer wants to know more than anything whether you are able to work well with others. So if you happen to be pursuing employment during a Venus retrograde, put your team-spirit face in plain view.

Tip 6 for Surviving Venus Retrograde: Escape from Negative People

A Venus retrograde serves an important purpose in making sure you are not denying your most accurate perceptions of someone to stay in an unrewarding relationship. The deeper your emotional attachment is to someone, the greater the chance it will fog your clarity about them. Every relationship has its ups and downs, as that is part of life. There really is no escaping this fact. Even experiencing some adversity and eventually working through it can strengthen the bond between two individuals. But what if you are always having your goals negated by someone, or are you having to deny what you really need to be happy just to stay with someone?

This is where a Venus retrograde can rescue you if you are a willing participant. You have to take the first step and really be honest with yourself. If there are friends and family members telling you that you are in a self-defeating relationship, there may be some truth in what they are observing. Letting go of a person you feel totally attached to takes some real determination. It is doing an about-face from your old self to embrace a new one. You have to realize that the other person may not be willing to change as long as you are seen as someone who can be manipulated. In an unintentional way, you are allowing the relationship to continue in a business-as-usual manner. You might even be hoping your partner will go through a personal transformation if you keep giving in to their wishes. The real problem is that you are not getting a fair deal.

A Venus retrograde will quickly reveal to you the reward for leaving a limiting relationship. If you make your departure under this cycle, you will feel a newfound freedom. Your mind will start seeing how you lacked equality. You will need to re-train yourself to look for healthier partnerships. You will have to constantly tell yourself there is no going back to someone who does not treat you as an equal. Venus is there to remind you to value your independence and to find people who do not fear your search for empowerment. Mutual love and admiration are really what you desire. When you leave a person who negates your true self, it is very liberating. It opens the door for the right person to come into your life.

Tip 7 for Surviving Venus Retrograde: Face Adversity

Venus is known as the peacemaker planet in astrology. This smooth-gliding celestial wanderer can guide you safely around difficult situations. Being the ambassador of getting adversaries to find a peaceful and agreeable settlement is part of the Venus mission statement. One potential drawback of a Venus retrograde is that you may be tempted to tiptoe around disagreements with others. It is fine to know when to avoid tension-provoking situations. Sometimes this is the best strategy, instead of getting caught up in skirmishes you don't need to join. An occasion might come along when you are better off initiating a dispute if it means defending your rights. It might be worth it in the long run to stand your ground, even if it takes you out of your comfort zone.

It has been said that feeling a little fear is not such a bad thing, as it means you can respond to a challenge when needed. But then again, too much fear may cause you to freeze in your tracks. You can get so stuck that there seems to be no way to move. This is like how some people describe a dream in which they are trying to run away from danger, but the harder they try to move their feet, the more they spin their wheels. It could be that you are not able to move through the tough obstacles and confrontations on your path. It is true that a Venus retrograde will often call on you to use good judgment in handling a crisis. You will need to decide how to fix the problem. Running away from it will only make it bigger. This may be hard to believe, but problems will disappear faster if you meet them head-on during a Venus retrograde. The key is that you have to be mentally and emotionally balanced. It is crucial not to let your moods swing so far out that you lose your clarity and make a problem worse than it is. If you back off and get your mental faculties in order to put a strategy together, a mountain standing in your way can be pushed aside. You may need to convince yourself to take that first step in dealing with a worrisome issue.

There is another thing to keep in mind when attempting to surmount an obstacle on your path during this retrograde cycle. You might need to get help from a friend, soulmate, or other ally to help you figure out the best solution to a dilemma. Venus has a team energy in its DNA. When you are in the midst of a Venus retrograde, putting someone else to work with you to face adversity may be just the right way to move. Knowing you are not alone may be the confidence booster you need to motivate yourself to slay the dragon. Don't tell yourself you are being too dependent on someone. There are times when a little help from your friends is what is needed to give you the confidence to look adversity straight in the eye. The payoff is that it will make you feel stronger. And don't worry—you won't lose your independence from getting another person's support.

Tip 8 for Surviving Venus Retrograde: Don't Get Trapped in the Past

A retrograde planet has a special energy to take you backward through time. It will get you to process memories over and over in unique ways. This does offer you a chance to discover insights you might have missed about events that happened in the near or distant past. Since Venus is such a strong relationship planet, you will have a tendency during its retrograde periods to reflect on your dealings with others. Some of what you remember may be wonderful memories that energize you when you recall them. There could also be memories that are not so pleasant. If you dwell on the past, you will remain stuck. Learning from past encounters with others is a great source of wisdom. It helps in current relationships not to repeat the same mistakes that were part of past relationships. Old, worn-out patterns won't do you much good when it comes to being happy in a relationship in the here and now.

Perhaps you have heard the term in psychology called *projection*. When you don't deal with or get clear about an inner issue, you are likely to project or think that another person you are involved with might be exhibiting this behavior. There is another side to projection as well. If you don't live out your own individual energies, there is the possibility of attracting people who are too egocentric. Venus retrogrades will aggravate this pattern if it is still too much a reality in your life at this time. Don't feel bad if this section rings a bell for you. Everyone has some quality they are working on even in the best relationship. The important thing to remember is that a Venus retrograde is not supposed to make your life unhappy. It might bring to the surface an issue you may need to work on. This might be a time of great insight for you and a path to harmony.

Venus has another key function in that it has an association with our olfactory nerves, or sense of smell. Your sense of smell is connected to parts of the brain linked to emotional memory. Olfactory memory refers to recollection of odors. Scientists have identified as many as one thousand smell receptors in the human body that find rebirth throughout a lifetime. A Venus retrograde has the capacity to greatly stimulate your senses, and that includes sensitivity to various odors. A particular odor could suddenly remind you of harmonious experiences that can be traced back to your past. Perhaps an odor reminds you of your mother's cooking or the childhood home that you enjoyed.

But what if you are surprised by an odor that takes you back to a memory you've long wanted to leave behind? Just remember to stay grounded and think positive. This will serve to keep you out of the grasp of a negative memory that you would just as soon not revisit. Don't despair. Even if a memory rubs you the wrong way or is upsetting, it still could be a learning experience. The key here is to integrate the emotions or feelings aroused into the present. You don't need to dwell on the memory. Dreams have a similar potential impact on a person. So if you are transported back into the past by an odor, just think that perhaps it was meant to happen. The universe may be revealing to you a deeper insight into that situation.

Believe it or not, a Venus retrograde could activate past-life relationship issues. A behavior could resurface, and you may wonder where it is coming from. For instance, you may grow angrier than usual. Your moods could be more unpredictable during the Venus retrograde time period. If you are an outgoing type, you may feel unusually quiet and want to retreat into a shell. All of these examples may be a signal that a past-life pattern is coming to your attention. An internal processing may be occurring that is helping you integrate this energy successfully into your life. Whether you have increased emotional outbursts or display a quieter side, it has to do with getting the insight to turn this past-life energy into creative self-expression. In other words, you are being given an opportunity to learn from past-life patterns and put these memories into a positive current-life experience. The bottom line is that you are getting empowered.

Tip 9 for Surviving Venus Retrograde: Stay Focused

Venus encourages you and everyone else to carefully consider options before putting a plan into action. This, you could say, is the normal manner in which Venus activates your thinking. This very considerate planet taps you on the shoulder or whispers in your ear to remind you to consider all choices in front of you. During a Venus retrograde, you may have to focus on one direction, even if it is painful at first to do so. Getting your concentration power into action will be required at times during a Venus retrograde. This is especially true if you have a serious goal to pursue. The world may call to you with many possibilities under a Venus retrograde. So many choices look like the right one. To get a plan accomplished, you will need to give yourself permission to ignore other possibilities and start moving forward, as difficult as this might be.

There will be friends and family with good intentions wanting you to join them in fun activities. This might actually be a good thing to help you relax. Taking a break from what you are concentrating on is good for your mind and physical well-being. Just be sure you don't conveniently escape with others too often, leaving your main goal undone. During a Venus retrograde, people may come out of the woodwork, or someone may need a shoulder to cry on. You could feel obligated to be of assistance. That's okay, but make sure you manage your time effectively or it will slip and slide away.

People may mean well by wanting to spend time with you. There is nothing wrong with having an active social life, which is being true to your Venusian instincts. But there are certain parameters to keep in mind to make sure you stay on schedule to finish what you start. There is no doubt that a Venus retrograde will activate the people connections in your life. Social media never looked so good as a way to run away from being focused on what you need to accomplish. So be sure to be disciplined enough to enjoy the best of all of your worlds. You do deserve to have some fun mixed in with work.

Staying committed to a goal plays right into making good use of your time. Rather than splitting your concentration in a diversified way, it may pay extra dividends to have one target to shoot at during this retrograde cycle. You will find it easier to stay on top of your game. This does not mean every Venus retrograde should be handled like this, but only that there could be one where you will find it easier to finish what you start by blocking out distractions. When this retrograde period ends, you can move more spontaneously into multiple directions if you choose. Multitasking will be easier if you get one major goal either finished or well on its way to being done. You will be proud of yourself.

Tip 10 for Surviving Venus Retrograde: Evaluate Your Work World

A Venus retrograde is a good time to go over your work goals as well as determine what you are already talented at doing. Venus likes to inspire you to put on a business hat as much as a relationship one. You may be happy with your current work situation or business you are operating. If you are thinking about making a change in your career aspirations, this cycle could be a motivating force to think about a plan, even if it is acted upon at a later date. People often have more abilities than they realize. You might want to list what you already know how to do. There may be a way to transfer this knowledge into a new position. There might be a need to get a life coach or simply ask for the advice of someone you trust. The stimulation from another person's assessment of your skills may help you brainstorm your way into a new opportunity. It may be a real challenge to step back objectively enough to take a look at your capabilities. A Venus retrograde could be the right time period to get some valuable input from a good ally.

If you are working at a place of employment where you want to ask for a raise, a Venus retrograde is probably not the most opportune time to do so. But you could put together a strategy as to why you think you deserve a raise. When Venus turns direct, you and an employer could then be more in sync. As the old saying goes, timing is everything.

If you own a business, a Venus retrograde is a great time to trim down what is no longer working. You could save money by ascertaining what is working for you and what is not. This six-week time period is possibly what you need to restructure your business operations. Do you need more employees or less? Perhaps new machinery is required that better keeps up with production and especially the quality and quantity needed to make ends meet. You can make more money by figuring out the most efficient method to fit the needs of the current time period. Economizing is a key Venus theme.

The layout or appearance of your place of business is important. Venus retrograde can guide you to add some style and color. Making people feel welcome is part of being a success, no matter what type of business you run. If you have a website or use social media, the same philosophy applies. The appearance is like an invitation to pull people into your business. It is a vibrant welcome sign. The content of whatever type of advertising you use may need a bit of a change. Even a business card may need a new look. Do you need a new photograph that best says who you are now? Venus retrograde has many artistic offerings to send your way to make your work more profitable.

Values are another Venus theme. You may find yourself wondering whether your current job matches your values. This may get you thinking about what type of work fits in with your ideals. It could be that you need to stay at your current job to pay the bills. You could find a volunteer role that satisfies your desire to live out part of your dream. There are a variety of possibilities to live out your highest beliefs.

Tip 11 for Surviving Venus Retrograde:
Be Careful with Major Purchases and Spending

Venus is very much connected to acquiring possessions. You could say this is one of its key functions in our lives. Buying minor things under a Venus retrograde will not get you in much trouble, but if you must buy something with a large price tag, make sure you know the return policy in case it does not work out the way you had hoped. Find a safe place for receipts, as they can mysteriously disappear during a retrograde visit of Venus. If there is no possibility of returning an item and it is a big expense, you may want to avoid making the purchase until after Venus turns direct. Why go against a strong current if you don't need to? There will be occasions when you can't wait because that is the way life presents itself to us at times. Emergencies happen that require fast responses. At these times, make sure you are getting the best deal possible and the quality is acceptable. Listen carefully to all of the details during a transaction. Sometimes it is wise to have another person accompany you on a complicated deal during Venus retrograde. The companion at your side may hear something you miss. It never hurts to have an extra pair of eyes and ears along for the ride.

If you have already been thinking about replacing a worn-out item before a Venus retrograde arrives, you will be one step ahead of the game. Even here, you need to exercise caution about committing to a major expense if you can wait. This is one time when delayed gratification is in your best interest. You will be happy later on that you waited.

Watch out when using credit cards. They look like free money until you get the bill. Venus retrograde may paint the illusion that you need to buy more than you need. This applies to taking out loans as well. If you must spend more money during a Venus retrograde, just be sure to search for the lowest interest rate possible. Watch out for investment opportunities as well. If something looks too good to be true, it likely will cause you trouble.

Do your research carefully if you are going to put your money into risky situations. It would be better to wait until Venus turns direct, because your thinking will be clearer. Debt can accumulate in a hurry during this six-week time period if you are not careful with your money. Even transferring a credit-card balance requires much discretion. It can be a great temptation to fill the card to the maximum once again. The point here is not to get carried away when using credit cards.

If you loan someone money or items during a Venus retrograde, there is a greater possibility you won't get it back. This won't bother you if it is a small amount of dollars or a possession easily replaced, but if you are lending large amounts of cash or big items, be careful. Think about what you can afford to lose. This does not mean you cannot or should not be generous with your resources. There is pleasure in giving. Just be a little more shrewd during this retrograde time period in how you decide to help others. It can be said as well that if you are doing the borrowing, try to return what is loaned to you. It will make your friends and family members trust you and be willing to help you out in the future.

How about people who know how to make you feel guilty until you give them your money or other resources on a regular basis? Be really careful during a Venus retrograde. You can get reeled in a lot easier than when Venus moves direct. You might appear to be a wonderful supply of free money, like a gift that does not stop giving. Know your limits. Tough love might be needed. You really will not be doing someone much good if you are always enabling dependent behavior. So the advice here is to create the right limits to be a generous person.

Tip 12 for Surviving Venus Retrograde: Keep Your Expectations Reasonable

During a Venus retrograde, it is wise to cherish every little success. To avoid feeling terribly disappointed, don't ask for more than life can deliver. There is a temptation to exaggerate your own abilities during this time period. "Keep it simple" is a wise mantra to repeat regularly. It is okay to challenge yourself to push beyond your comfort zones. You might be the type of person who will tempt the odds no matter what people around you advise you to do. Nobody is saying to be less than you should be. Just be more pragmatic during a Venus retrograde to get the most mileage out of this time period.

Try to be reasonable about what you look for in others during a Venus retrograde. They might be doing the best they can. There is often a tendency during this cycle to think others are capable of doing extraordinary things for you. If you expect someone to finish something by a deadline, make sure to get whatever they need to them way ahead of time. Delays are often part of a Venus retrograde cycle. Time does not always cooperate the way you hope it will. So to be on the safe side, be sure to give yourself extra time to get things done according to the needs of a plan.

Finding agreeable ways to work with others toward a goal could be challenging. Don't be surprised if you and a person have a different perspective on how to begin and finish a project. Patience with each other helps to see the other's point of view. Fighting for your own ideas without trying to compromise will prove unfruitful. Try to let each other know that your concepts are being taken into consideration. You will enjoy working together that much more and will likely produce an end result that is pleasing to both of you. It may be that your individual visions of a goal are not as distant as you think. Finding that midpoint will make each of you feel better about working as a team.

Watch how far you go in trying to make someone happy or pleased with you. Don't paint such a rosy picture of what you might be able to do for a person, as it might be hard to deliver this in a Venus retrograde. It is wonderful to raise the spirits of a friend or lover who needs your help. This is a great thing to do for them. It is in trying to promise the impossible that you will disappoint them, so be aware of your limits,

Tip 13 for Surviving Venus Retrograde: Preserve Your Personal Power

Maintaining a sense of empowerment during a Venus retrograde may come down to tuning in to peaceful tranquility. This allows for your mental and creative drive to stay at a high operating level. Stress may be all around you, and yet serenity is one pleasant nearby escape. It does not mean you can't have a strong disagreement with someone. This is a normal part of life. What you don't need are people visiting your home who disturb your mental and emotional equilibrium. Keeping a sense of inner harmony will prove essential to your happiness during this cycle.

Venus retrograde could push you to be more introspective. This is not meant to interfere with your everyday functioning but more to enrich your inner being. This could be a time when you are trying to make your life simpler in a very complex modern world. Balancing the demands of a job or other responsibilities can be taxing on your nervous system. One key place to preserve your well-being is your living environment.

Doing your favorite things at home to stay calm is a way to reward yourself. Life is hard work. If you are a parent, that adds extra responsibility. A job puts pressure on you to perform at maximum capacity. The plus of a Venus retrograde is that it stimulates brainstorming material to find ways to keep problems at bay. It is not that you want to run away from dealing with issues that arise, but more that you need to make sure you don't get lost in them. You can easily lose your sense of personal empowerment when your mind gets totally burned out. It can happen quickly during a Venus retrograde because you might let down your defenses. You can simply forget to preserve your energy level. Pushing yourself to do one more job function, even though your body is saying it is time to quit, may result in feeling powerless. Your creative punch is weakened in going way beyond the call of duty on a regular basis. It is vital to remember that Venus is all about keeping your life balanced.

Doing whatever it takes to have a home that feels safe is the main thing. It can be a place where you feel comfortable resting and at the same time where you entertain people you care about. The social flair of Venus is never far from your imagination. You will enjoy your social interactions that much more when you feel inwardly centered. Having a healing type of home atmosphere that is a wonderful sanctuary from stress is good for your mind, body, and soul.

In many ways your health and your sense of feeling empowered are greatly interconnected. When you are taking good care of your body, your mind will naturally feel centered and focused. Your creative power is stronger when your diet and exercise are well planned. You don't need to have a perfect diet or run a marathon. The main idea during a Venus retrograde is to avoid extremes. Eating balanced meals and getting a little exercise during a Venus retrograde cycle will do wonders for your vitality and keep your outlook on life brighter.

Venus represents the arts. During a Venus retrograde, wearing clothes with colors that lift your spirits can be empowering. In a work space or your residence, having items such as paintings that stimulate your mental power could be another plus. It might be that listening to your favorite music generates a soothing feeling that puts you on top of the world. Reaching out to those things that symbolize in your own mind a sense of personal power during a Venus retrograde is true wisdom.

When you are feeling positive in your mental attitude, it will attract good things. Abundance will be more likely to come to you. Your attracting power to bring supportive people and an overall harmony into your life is the reward for seeing the cup half full. When you pay special attention to nourishing your self esteem during a Venus retrograde, good fortune is never far away.

Tip 14 for Surviving Venus Retrograde: Don't Create Unnecessary Friction

During a Venus retrograde, you might think you need to create tension with other people just because you feel motivated to do so. What may cause this to occur? It may sound strange, but you could be having a problem accepting peace. This sometimes happens during Venus retrogrades. The natural rhythm of Venus encourages you to seek calmness and various forms of relaxation. If you grow bored with this, there can be a tendency to overreact and exhibit actions that are very disruptive. This may not sound like you, and it could very well be true that you don't usually act this way. Don't feel like you are the only person who reacts to a Venus retrograde in this manner. There may be many individuals at the same moment in time wondering why they are behaving in ways that are not typical of them.

An inner restlessness can intensify during this retrograde cycle. This is not a bad thing. It is just sending you a signal that you have extra energy. The key thing to remember is to put this vitality to productive use. There is a divine discontent that sometimes appears during a Venus retrograde. It could be a real challenge to be happy with what you have, even if your life is going in a great direction. Be careful not to think that situations should be more perfect. A partner, a job, or your life in general may not appear to be living up to your expectations. A Venus retrograde sometimes paints the illusion that something is wrong, when in reality it is a good situation for you. Make sure you do some sound reality testing before making a major change during a Venus retrograde. It may be wise to get a second opinion from a reliable person.

Venus tries to get you to accept stability. Balancing a drive to exert your will with knowing when to be patient is a potential challenge during a Venus retrograde. When you tune in to the energy of a Venus retrograde cycle, it is within your grasp to enjoy both taking action and knowing when to take a restful timeout. You can muster up the initiative to put out your best effort to get a job done and know when to pause. There is no need to grow frustrated.

Symptoms that you are struggling with the flow of Venus retrograde include starting unnecessary arguments. Reacting angrily for no real reason to another person's ideas is another possibility. Blaming others for a problem you started is yet another indication you are having trouble during this retrograde time period.

If you are causing disputes with others just to spice up your life, there are ways to get around this. Channeling your energy into productive outlets is the best thing to do. When you see you are getting positive results from your actions, it will help you maintain a more even temperament. If you can calm yourself down, whether through talking about how you feel or simply getting some distance from a situation, it will help you feel not as emotionally intense. There is a lot of creative power embedded in a Venus retrograde that you can learn to use to your advantage.

There may be times when you need to cultivate patience. If you make decisions with insight, it is far better than letting impulse always be in the driver's seat. Venus is a strong relationship planet. Listen with a willingness to hear the needs of those closest to you to maintain harmony in these relationships. This will allow you to ride out some of the tension between you during a Venus retrograde.

Tip 15 for Surviving Venus Retrograde:
Maintain a Flexible Attitude

During a Venus retrograde, there can be a tendency to circle the wagons and hold on to rigid ideas. If you grow too defensive, you might alienate your closest allies. Stay as open as you can. There is nothing to fear. Why might you feel the need to keep a firm grip on an idea at all costs? During Venus retrograde, you can feel extra suspicious of change. It seems to come with the territory. In some ways you might be better off not making a drastic change during a Venus retrograde. You need to exercise care when it comes to being open to the opinions of others. You don't have to agree with them, but if you are receiving good advice about a situation, it will pay off to listen. So don't be afraid to experiment with considering alternative ideas. They may pay off in ways you had not considered previously. A Venus retrograde can bring you a new surprise that you may be happy to have allowed to happen.

Venus is associated with our values as well as our likes and dislikes. There is a temptation to be strongly possessive of our favorite value judgments about life. Being flexible will turn out to be a winner for you in the long run. It could open the door to opportunities you had not imagined. If you remain headstrong in one direction during a Venus retrograde, you could miss out on walking into a more abundant set of circumstances. There might be a new friendship or job presenting itself to you. If you don't stubbornly resist a new experience, there could be greater joy coming right into your life.

So keep your eyes and ears at least a little bit open to new possibilities. There is nothing wrong with holding on to what has worked for you in the past. But mixing the past with something different may result in a more expansive and rewarding opportunity. Just think of it as there being a magical door that might just swing wide open and invite you in for a wonderful new event.

Tip 16 for Surviving Venus Retrograde: Build Social Capital

You don't want to let yourself feel completely isolated from getting the support you need during a Venus retrograde. There is a tendency to pull back from others during this retrograde cycle. This runs contrary to the wonderful social connections Venus encourages you to form with others. In other words, you need to make sure you make a strong attempt to create valuable partnerships that enrich your life. If you are a very sociable person, it is true that you may not choose to spend more time by yourself. But there is nothing wrong with recharging your battering by getting some downtime. Then again, if you need to enhance your opportunities by joining forces with a group or individuals wanting to help you move forward, then this might be a key time period in which to do this.

You could find yourself reflecting on who you can really count on when you need to get through a challenge. This is a natural instinct that gets triggered during Venus retrogrades. This can be a reality-check type of time interval. You are attempting to determine ahead of time who may be the right person to help you deal with particular situations if they should arise. In other words, you are wanting to be well prepared for whatever challenge might present itself. What you don't want to do is think you can't trust anyone. That would be working against yourself.

A Venus retrograde can guide you to seek out new alliances. Friendships can be formed that stimulate creative living. Being around upbeat people lifts your spirits and gives you the confidence to seek greater abundance. Having a wide range of social or even business contacts helps open new options. Having reliable people around you increases your chances for success.

If you extend your generosity to people they will be more likely to do the same for you. This is a way of building social capital that will come through for you when you need it. Riding the waves of Venus energy that help you reach out to people aids you in creating strong bonds with others.

Venus Turning Direct:
The Jet Lag Following the Venus Retrograde

When Venus finishes its six-week retrograde movement, you may let out a sigh of relief. Your overall grasp of social interactions will likely start to get into a more natural flow. People seem to pick up on your ideas faster. You don't need to explain your wants and dislikes with as much persistence. Your goals for the future might seem easier to attain than when you were trying to survive Venus retrograde, or maybe those future plans seem to fit better with your values now. A small celebration could be in order for persevering while Venus was in retrograde motion. It is not a bad idea, after a Venus retrograde ends, to have a type of joyous ritual. This could be going to your favorite restaurant or being with the friends you most enjoy having in your life. It isn't so much to mark the end of a negative time period but more to remind yourself that it is time to launch forward.

As you take a look back down memory lane, perhaps you will realize that you did gain a new understanding about some significant relationships. The tremendous influence of a Venus retrograde to get you to take an honest look at your closest partnerships may still be getting rearranged in your mind. In some ways you might feel as though certain insights about a person are getting tossed around like clothes in a dryer. You might be wondering if other people feel the same way. They probably are but may not be expressing it in words. In the first days of Venus moving direct, you may not be so sure of what you are processing internally. Don't worry. It will eventually make sense. There is often a feeling of fatigue when Venus begins to turn direct. To some extent everyone undergoes a similar transition as Venus moves out of its retrograde cycle back into direct motion. So try to remember to be patient with those you are closest to. They too are making the same adjustments to this new Venus gravitational pull. In some ways it is like being in a state of limbo as Venus starts its direct takeoff. You may be so focused on your own reentry to Venus direct that you lose sight of the fact that others are doing the same thing. It may not be as apparent that people you encounter in all phases of your life just came out of a Venus retrograde, but rest assured that everyone is trying to take what they reflected on during Venus retrograde and move forward.

You may not have missed a beat in getting your goals accomplished while Venus was retrograde, but more than likely you did reevaluate a relationship or what you value in life on some level. It could be that as you embrace the Venus direct cycle you will be putting something learned during the retrograde time period to work for you. It may take some time to tune in to this information, but sooner or later you will. Since Venus is very much a people-oriented planet, it may be that interactions with people will awaken what you did learn during Venus retrograde on a more conscious level as you live your life in the Venus direct movement.

The first couple of days following a Venus retrograde could be somewhat disorienting. Your mind and body are trying to get into sync with this energy shift. It is similar to jet lag following a long plane trip. If you feel a tendency to slow down, don't be concerned. Your momentum will pick up quickly as you get into the flow of the Venus direct rhythm. It is okay to rest more if you need to when Venus first resumes direct motion. If you have projects or a job to perform, not pressuring yourself to be in a big rush can bring you right into a Venus direct faster. In other words, you tend to land on your feet more quickly when experiencing less anxiety. If you see yourself getting duties accomplished, whether at home or at work, it has a great grounding impact to help you tune in to Venus moving from retrograde to direct that much more quickly. Even getting some exercise helps with this adjustment. Connecting with physical energy seems to realign your mind with getting business done as usual.

It isn't necessarily possible to predict just how you might respond to each Venus retrograde. Any misstep can be corrected, and this is important to remember. There is always the chance you did not feel that out of sorts in all areas of your life while Venus was retrograde. If you did have trouble connecting with certain people during the Venus retrograde, you very well may be socially ready for any type of action as soon as Venus goes direct again. During some Venus retrogrades, your energy will build for the entire six weeks, ready to pounce powerfully when Venus resumes direct motion. There could be a Venus retrograde that sent your life into a backward somersault. Your job, finances, or a relationship issue may have been extra challenging. Changes may have occurred that you did not expect to happen. These are those Venus retrogrades that could stall your forward momentum for a short period of time as you find your bearings again when Venus turns direct. But if you make wise choices, you can transform any adversity that you encountered during the Venus retrograde into a winning point. You will need to stay positive in your thinking and make use of your closest friends so the energetic atmosphere greeting you from Venus direct can take you to new horizons.

Correcting Missteps During a Venus Retrograde

You will likely realize during a Venus retrograde that you took a wrong step. You could be right in the middle of getting a job done. It is nearly impossible to avoid redoing some things during a retrograde time period. It happens to everyone. Don't let this bother you. It might be that you come up with a better plan to get a goal finished in a less stressful and even more time-saving way. Be happy if you come to an understanding of a better path to take. During a retrograde planet's movement, it is common for your mind to see alternative options. They may or may not be better than your original choice, but there is always the possibility that you will see a winning formula you had not considered.

The economizing energy of Venus can guide you on how to get your needs met in ways that better fit your budget. If you run into indecisiveness that aggravates your nervous system, then you might need to take a brief timeout. Give yourself permission to do this. Take the time to allow your mind and emotions to find balance. Otherwise your mind will feel like it is stuck. Do something enjoyable if that is what it takes to keep you from worrying excessively about the outcome of a situation. Don't force a decision if it just doesn't seem right. The end result won't be pleasing if you are making choices under great duress. There are times when you will have to push forward during a Venus retrograde because time is of the essence. If this is the case, it would serve you well to find a moment or two to escape the pressure of a key decision so you can make a successful landing. Sometimes just getting even a small amount of distance will allow you to determine the best choice. Venus has a way of suggesting just the right atmosphere to get you into the correct mental framework to think clearly. This might be a restaurant, a movie theater, the relaxing atmosphere in your house, a nature walk, or another one of your favorite ways to stay calm.

Relationship issues may need to be reexamined during a Venus retrograde. Revisiting a better way to get what you need in a partnership can be accomplished successfully during this Venus six-week cycle. The trick is negotiating from a position of strength and at the same time creating win-win situations. Being able to objectively see both sides of an issue is actually easier to do when you embrace the wisdom embedded in Venus. It does require some patience, which can be a real challenge at times. When you show you are considering not only your side of a disagreement but the other person's as well, it will reduce the tension. You will find the harmony you desire faster when being tolerant of opposing viewpoints. You don't have to totally surrender your own needs. Venus retrograde is a good duration of time in which to work out differences and for you and another person to come to a favorable agreement. Being diplomatic does not require you to be a doormat for others to walk on. It means you can be assertive without having to be totally demanding. A compromise could be closer than you think. It might require flexibility from you and the person with whom you are working out a problem.

Your insights into how you interact with others can find a new clarity. If there is a particular pattern you want to change in your social behavior, this retrograde cycle can help you do this. Maybe recently you tried too hard to please someone.

This is your chance to be more self-confident and see that you don't need to act in this manner. You can be yourself. With a lot of practice, you can feel renewed. If you were too demanding, this is your opportunity to be less pushy to get your own way. You can be assertive without being too demanding. A Venus retrograde is a great cycle to practice your skills in working toward solutions that are mutually beneficial. It gets easier as you more consciously try to adopt this behavior. It will bring a person closer to you in mind and spirit. Trust certainly deepens, which is a nice reward.

You may be regretting a business decision that was made during a Venus retrograde. This planet does have a financial influence in its symbolism. There is an earthy and pragmatic dimension to Venus that must be acknowledged. Perhaps you were overconfident in taking on too big of a job. You may need to discuss this with an employer or a coworker. Once again, you need to wear a Venusian diplomatic hat. You may need to plead your case, but be sure to define this on a business level. If you keep your emotions out of the talk, you will probably get a better deal for yourself. Wait for the right time to talk, when you feel mentally sharp. Make it clear that you are aware of the other person's concerns. If you have your own business, you could realize you did not ask for enough money or time for a job to be finished. Approaching a client once again could be tricky, but if you make your needs clear, you might be able to reach a fair agreement. Remember to be reasonable. You might not get your entire wish list fulfilled, but getting some of it attained is still a positive. It is always wise before a Venus retrograde to be as clearminded as possible about financial business. Emotions about money and possessions do get intensified during some Venus retrogrades.

If you must attempt to fix a misstep during a Venus retrograde, don't panic. When you stay mentally centered, the road to success is usually closer than you think. There is a problem-solving instinct in a Venus retrograde that will often come through for you. This peacemaker of the sky will point out the secrets to create winning negotiation formulas in magical ways. This is part of this planet's job resumé, so let it work for you.

Positive and Negative Ways to Experience a Venus Retrograde	
Positive Expression	*Negative Expression*
Good negotiator	Too compromising
Decisiveness	Indecisiveness
Seeking harmony in relationships	Creating unnecessary conflict
Balanced relationships	Unrealistic expectations
Clarity in career and work goals	Lack of ambition
Solid self-assuredness	Looking for too much approval

This is a short review of some of the most challenging themes of a Venus retrograde. Remember that anything you are struggling with during these six Venus retrograde weeks can be turned into a winning experience.

A Venus retrograde is an opportunity to put your negotiating skills into action. There is a chance you could be overly accommodating when trying to get the fairest deal for yourself. If you become too compromising, your life won't be as enjoyable. It will feel like you are always accepting second best. So keep in mind that getting your own way once in a while is a wise policy.

Venus retrogrades will find you wondering at times why you are having trouble making decisions, even if you usually act on impulse. Your intuition could be less sharp. Indecisiveness is nerve-wracking if it goes on for too long. You may find it better to live with a decision than remain motionless for prolonged time periods. Venus is the planet constantly getting us to weigh choices to ascertain which are the best. Learning from the experience of believing in your decisions will probably make you happier in the long run. You can always tweak a choice to make it better meet your needs.

Relationships are a major part of the Venus world. A Venus retrograde can seem like an obstacle course at times in maintaining harmony with others. Working with lovers, coworkers, or friends to solve a problem might be more tension-provoking than normal during a Venus retrograde. Having patience with yourself and others is a good place to start in getting to a win-win situation. It is easier to resolve conflict if you can communicate what you need from someone. Listening with an open mind is another thing to consider to bring about positive results. If you focus more on what will bring about unity rather than dwell on your differences, you will be well on your way to finding a peaceful solution to a problem.

Venus retrogrades can suddenly throw a relationship out of balance. What seemed like an equal partnership may feel like you are denying your own goals. Then again, if you have unrealistic expectations of someone, happiness is not going to be your reality. Don't look for perfection. A give and take is essential during a Venus retrograde. A soulmate will remain close if you stay reasonable in what you need from them. You will feel more valued if a partner gives you the attention you need and deserve.

Work goals can grow sleepy during a Venus retrograde. You may need to push yourself harder to meet a deadline. It may be just as important to have a reward in mind to encourage you to finish what you set out to do. Ambition is more challenging to sustain during a Venus retrograde. If you are seeking a more rewarding job or a new career path, don't let a Venus retrograde dampen your enthusiasm. Every great goal often meets up with a delay. Think of a Venus retrograde as an opportunity to clarify your serious plans for the future. Your body and mind could be asking you to pace yourself better during this retrograde. You can be very successful at balancing ambition and rest.

Believe in what you value during a Venus retrograde. If you look for too much approval from others, it will stall your most cherished plans for an abundant life. Teamwork is fine, and seeking advice from others sometimes is a motivating force to accomplish a goal. Just remember not to let someone easily talk you out of an idea.

Venus Stationary Motion

When Venus appears to be standing still when viewed from the earth, it is referred to as having stationary movement. This motionless appearance occurs when the Venus orbit is about to reverse its movement either from direct to retrograde (called stationary retrograde) or from retrograde to direct (called stationary direct). In reality, Venus does not change direction or stop moving. It just paints the illusion that this is going on in the sky. The standing still is known as a planet's station. A Venus station (when it remains motionless) lasts for two days when it is about to change direction either from retrograde to direct or from direct to retrograde.

When Venus is preparing to move from direct to retrograde motion and is in a stationary stance for two days, it is important to carefully consider any decisions that will impact your relationships. You may feel hesitant and less sociable during these days. Think of this as a cooling-down period to reflect carefully before promising too much to others. If you find yourself indecisive, it could be in your best interest to wait a few days to see if you feel clearer. The outcomes of your decisions are likelier to give you the results you want. Even doing business in the world may not seem as flowing during this Venus stationary retrograde movement. Your negotiating skills, even if normally sharp, might be slightly duller until Venus turns direct. If you don't need to make major relationship or business decisions during these couple of days, the best policy is to wait. In the long run, it might save you a lot of anxiety and even money. Do some fun and relaxing activities instead. Give yourself permission to escape from too much responsibility. Try it and you will like it.

When Venus is ready to move from retrograde to direct motion and remains stationary direct for two days, you can feel this anticipation with great force. All of a sudden any waiting tendencies on your part can quickly evaporate. It is as though a fog has lifted. You may be more ready to enter a new relationship or to make new friends. You arrive at decisions more quickly. Business instincts are in full bloom. You will be wondering why you were so tentative while Venus was fully retrograde. Your self-confidence points you to fulfilling life paths. The little problems no longer seem so big, and large conflicts are easier to resolve. Peace and harmony are easier to achieve.

The Silver Lining Following a Venus Retrograde

Is there a light at the end of the Venus retrograde tunnel that feels like a reward for just getting through these six anxiety-filled weeks? Even if you think your life was turned upside down in countless ways, there was something given to you as a gift. What might that be? Try to think of the six weeks traveling in a Venus retrograde as a *sharpening of your social and business instincts.* It might not make sense to hear this right as Venus begins moving in direct motion again. This will become more apparent when Venus has been in direct motion for maybe a week or two. It may even be part of your reality in the first two days of Venus being in direct movement.

A new type of self-confidence in how you carry yourself in relationships and business can develop. The energy in a Venus retrograde takes you deeper within yourself and can strengthen your relationships. It brings to the surface any real relationship issues, even if they are difficult to face. The payoff is that you get to more clearly assess what you need from others in order to be happy. There can be an enriched feeling about your relationships because of your new insights.

Not long after a Venus retrograde ends, it might begin to sink in just how much you were starting to absorb in getting emotionally stronger. Balancing your mind and feelings becomes easier as you process those weeks when Venus was retrograde. As Venus begins to turn direct, it is possible that you could feel stronger internally. Your way of handling business in the world can reveal a new sense of personal power. The world may seem like it is responding faster to your goals. This may be due to your self-esteem rising to higher levels.

What you value in life may deepen or at least get redefined. It might simply be a minor adjustment in the way you relate to others that points the way to harmony. Your instincts to market your job skills can intensify. Attracting the abundance you need can become a talent. Old relationship patterns that no longer serve a useful purpose can be discarded. This gives you a liberated feeling. A more independent attitude in being yourself may be displayed. The choices that might have gotten lost in the turbulent, indecisive winds of a Venus retrograde may now transform into decisive forward movement. A more determined attitude to reward yourself can blossom. Finding a sense of inner peace is soothing to your mind, body, and soul. Your decisiveness creates a bolder path forward. With a revitalized self-confidence, you refuse to settle for less than you could become.

Chapter Four

Mars:
The Warrior Planet

Areas Influenced by Mars: Initiating action, expressing anger, competitiveness, identity
Elements Associated with Mars: Fire and water
Signs Ruled by Mars: Aries and its co-ruler of Scorpio
Mars Retrograde Gifts: Renewed vitality and a greater sense of capability
Duration of Mars Retrograde Cycle: Two months

Let's take a look at Mars moving direct before we consider its retrograde cycle. Mars provides us with tremendous physical energy. It embodies the spirit of competition. There was some important research done on the astrological charts of athletes by Michel Gauquelin, a French psychologist and statistician. Gauquelin studied the charts of thousands of athletes and discussed the Mars influence in his book *Cosmic Influences on Human Behavior.* He found that Mars was a strong planet in each chart in a remarkable statistical way. In anyone's life, including your own, this fiery planet lights a spark to act on creative impulses. Moving forward fearlessly is powered by the dynamic thrust of Mars energy.

Mars is the ruler of the fire sign Aries and is considered the co-ruler of watery Scorpio. Until the discovery of Pluto in 1930, Mars was the sole ruler of Scorpio. It is the Aries connection to Mars that is your call to action when you sense it is time to move on an idea or goal. It is the Mars link to Scorpio that at times will find you trying to be absolutely sure before you make that final decision to go for it. Both dimensions of Mars are important tools for you to put to good use.

Courage will be stimulated by Mars. This is often a spontaneous event. You might look back at actions you took and wonder where the daredevil attitude to get something accomplished came from. You may even feel as though you were scared into responding to a challenge. Without a doubt the clues will lead back to Mars. This planet denotes your inner smoke alarm that makes a loud sound to let you know if a situation is dangerous to enter. Or at least it is the planet that makes you wonder if you should enter where "angels fear to tread." There are those times when this adventurous planet will encourage you to throw caution to the wind. Your mind will tell you there is nothing to lose in taking a risk. Bravery colors your aura.

The Mars association with Scorpio offers a chance to channel the energy of this enterprising planet into business pursuits. If you need an adrenaline rush to work long hours or to get a work assignment finished, you can count on this planet to provide you with relentless energy. This is a naturally caffeinated planet that can propel you forward through any challenges. The inner drive to increase your wealth to make your life more rewarding is aided by Mars.

In mythology Mars was known as the god of war. Defeating enemies to defend the homeland was part of the Mars symbolism. Acquiring new territory through foreign conquests could be said to be part of the Mars legacy. Even in modern times Mars still triggers this combative tendency. Fighting for survival or just being warlike is in the Mars repertoire. There may be times when you will feel the need to defend your ideas with a fiery passion. Mars will stimulate your mind to be direct in making a strong statement about your ideas.

Being assertive to get your needs met is yet another Mars trait. Call it the desire to feel your own personal power. The point of this is not necessarily to overpower others but more to make sure you make progress in getting your own goals off the ground and well on their way to success. This can feel good and clarify your identity. Your need to show the world what you can do is raised to a high level by the industrious Mars energy.

Mars is linked to expressing anger. There really is no getting away from this. Anger is a natural emotion and is part of life. Tuning in to this dynamic force is clearly essential to establishing harmony. It does not do you any good to hide your anger because it only will build up inside of you with tremendous force. It may then come out in an explosive way that you never intended to happen. Your happiness will take a hit you don't need. So being honest with yourself when you are upset about something could be in your best interest. Letting those closest to you express their own anger is a wise policy. Usually it will bring you closer to solving problems in the long run.

There is a territorial side of Mars. What does this mean for you? Mars says it is okay to stake your own claim to your life pursuits. There comes a point when you realize your own goals must be pursued to energize your life. There is no time for boredom in the world of Mars. Restlessness is embedded into the pulse of this fiery celestial wanderer. Without Mars, there is a chance we would all be couch potatoes with little interest in pursuing our favorite interests in life.

It is true that a little patience might be required to get the best results, but at the same time you can't wait forever for the perfect time to launch an idea. There will be moments when courage summons you to act now. There is an urgency to put a plan into motion. Mars enjoys watching you take its fiery spirit and adopt it as part of your own nature to live your life to the fullest. There is no time like the present, according to the Mars doctrine. You might be accused of being too self-centered at times when playing your Mars card. It may be true that you need to be careful not to lose sight of those who might need your support for their own dreams and hopes for a better future. There is room enough for you and those you love to have your mutual goals realized.

Sexual drive is another Mars theme. Enjoying and exploring your sexuality is part of the Mars universe. The pursuit of a compatible partner on the physical and adventure levels is included in the Mars package. Finding a person you enjoy sharing passion with is stimulated by the Mars effect. While we are on the subject of passion, it should be said that this same energy can be directed into your work aspirations as well. Mars awakens the drive for sex for sure, but in addition it pushes you to explore your creative talents too. When you find subjects of interest, the Mars excitement will become elevated. Your self-confidence rises often when pursuing your dreams. Mars says don't look back when you find things you love doing.

There are a multitude of ways Mars can come into your life. This is the planet that fills you with the enthusiasm to put your ideas into action. You will often attract the attention of Mars when putting a plan into motion. This planet will show you how to make the best of what you intend to accomplish.

Your Sun Sign, Your Sign Element, and Mars Retrograde: A Dynamic Triad

If you read the previous Mercury and Venus chapters, it was explained how your Sun sign, in being associated with one of the four elements, will lead you to interact with a planet's retrograde movement in a unique manner. Your Sun sign is a very influential factor in your life. It is associated with one of the four elements: fire, earth, air, and water. Your Sun sign will connect with a Mars retrograde in correlation with your own element. You will not predictably respond to each Mars retrograde in the same way.

The element discussions that follow are meant to serve as a guide to help you understand how a Mars retrograde time period will work with you. This combined energy of your Sun sign and its corresponding element join forces with a Mars retrograde to open new experiences for you to encounter. The three unify to help you determine choices that are best for you to act on with confidence. How you embody your ideals and most fiery enthusiasm may grow more reflective during a Mars retrograde. It might not be that you are unsure of yourself. It could be that you need to use this time to clarify the right direction to pursue to make the most of your efforts. The motivation may be to save you time and energy.

You really are a mixture of the four elements, as this is true for all of us. The elements filter into your psychological nature and in the way you like to express yourself. Your Sun sign is a key component of your inner drive to show the world your capability. Even if you are new to astrology, just in knowing your own Sun sign element you are well on your way to knowing yourself on a deep level. In knowing your Sun's element you can begin to better tune in to the messages of a Mars retrograde time period. Your survival mode will turn on more quickly to handle whatever comes your way during this Mars retrograde cycle. What follows are brief descriptions of how your Sun sign and element mix with a Mars retrograde.

The Fire Signs (Aries, Leo, Sagittarius) and Mars Retrograde

If your Sun sign is a member of the fire element, your spontaneity might feel slightly slowed down during a Mars retrograde. Don't feel bad. This is a common occurrence for a fiery soul in trying to walk with the rhythm of this unusual Mars cycle. Your usual direct fashion of dealing with life may be skewed by Mars moving in backward motion. It might even be that you are wanting to get right to the point with someone and it is the other person acting with much hesitation. It might seem like they are dodging your questions. Try to be patient.

This is a two-month retrograde planetary trek in the sky that tries everyone's patience. It may not be every day during a Mars retrograde that you feel frustrated in your daily activities. Since Mars does remain retrograde for at least two months, you probably can't wait to make business or other important decisions. Events you want to attend or make happen can't always be put aside until a retrograde finally ends. If you move slower when feeling out of sorts, you will likely find it is easier to stay on target toward getting your goals accomplished.

It may sound like a contradiction, but there will be certain hours or days during this retrograde cycle when you will sense that you need to push on even if you are met with some resistance. Your inner strength and possibly your physical energy may get challenged, but if you persevere, you can still get a job done. If you find that it makes more sense not to act on an idea, you will more than likely find it easier to move forward swiftly when Mars does turn direct again. Because you are a fire sign, the waiting might seem painful, but in the end you will be rewarded. Your energy will be easier to launch powerfully early on when Mars goes direct again. At that time planet Earth will seem to be spinning more favorably, the way you like it.

If your Sun sign is fiery Aries (March 20–April 19), your usual way of acting out your everyday life may not seem to be going the way to which you are accustomed. The key thing to remember is that it is okay if you need to pause more before acting on an idea. This often does happen during a Mars retrograde, especially for you. Why? Because Mars is the planet that rules your Aries Sun sign. So generally speaking you are often going to be more sensitive to its moving from direct to retrograde and then back to direct again.

Since you have a natural affinity to Mars, it does give you an edge in responding to its retrograde cycle. If you have to move with a little more caution or reflection, it can help you consolidate your energy with greater focus. You could be pleasantly surprised that you are getting more done in a shorter amount of time. Patience will keep you from going in circles and getting no results. You may be more sensitive to criticism during a Mars retrograde. Try not to overreact if someone questions your decisions. It is okay to defend your ideas. Just be cognizant of the opinions of others. There is always the chance that outside advice may help make your life run more smoothly, especially during a Mars retrograde.

If your Sun sign is fiery Leo (July 22–August 22), you might be just as determined to put a plan to work during a Mars retrograde but with greater awareness of what impact you may have on others. During this two-month cycle, Mars could put you into a slower pace, allowing people to catch up to you. Your tendency is to be a leader, and this is a chance to tune in to whether those trying to follow you are really on the same page. Your desire to get noticed for something you want to make more visible may need an extra push during a Mars retrograde. It can seem like the universe is testing you to see if you can walk your talk. Then again, if you find you are trying to force things to happen, you may need to exercise patience. Don't be surprised if your normal physical stamina is not as strong and you need to pace yourself. Waiting for the best time to communicate your needs to others is not always something you excel at. Be sure you consider the opinions of those closest to you as much as your own during a Mars retrograde. It is the surest way to find harmony in your relationships.

If your Sun sign is fiery Sagittarius (November 21–December 21), your adventurous spirit may be toned down during a Mars retrograde. It isn't that you won't necessarily be as quick to jump on an opportunity as usual, but it is more likely you will take an extra glance before taking a leap of faith. That drive to be expansive will likely be a bit narrower during this cycle. This could turn out to have positive results in helping you find greater focus. Since you tend to get bored easily, Mars retrograde will help you keep your mind on a target with greater accuracy, meaning you could find this a very productive time period.

If you find that you feel somewhat disoriented, it is likely due to feeling somewhat scattered by moving in too many directions at the same time, which is always tempting for a Sagittarius. Staying centered is a wise strategy if your mind starts to race faster than you want it to. Communicate your needs honestly and you won't be frustrated. Even if you don't get all of your hopes and wishes agreed to, at least you will feel better that you said what was needed. If you are feeling very restless, you will need to exercise your mind and body. Mars moving in retrograde motion can stir up your nervous system perhaps more than some of the other signs. This is likely a signal that you need to channel your energy into productive outlets. With a little extra determination you can do this.

The Air Signs (Gemini, Libra, Aquarius) and Mars Retrograde

If your Sun sign is a member of the air element, a Mars retrograde might seem at times like it is blowing your ideas right back in your face. Don't despair. A lot of other people may be having a similar experience. It could be a good time to think of other alternatives to getting a goal accomplished. Your mind likes to be inquisitive. Mars normally speeds up your thought processes and provides fresh new insights. It can do the same thing during a retrograde trek of this fiery planet. The trick is to adapt your mental impulses to the energy of this cycle, which does not operate like you are accustomed to.

That cool, breezy approach you take to life might appear disrupted. There will be days during a Mars retrograde when you simply will need to push forward whether it feels right or not. Then again, if it seems like you are beating your head against a wall and not getting things done, you may need to take a break. It might sound strange, but you may need to distract yourself if you are not making any progress. Do your exercise routines, talk to a friend, walk the dog, read, play with your cat, go out for a meal, or indulge in something to take your mind off your concerns, then come back when refreshed. This often is the best way to deal with a Mars retrograde. Your energy will recharge when you stop thinking about what is not getting done. This can be a productive time period.

The good news is that when Mars turns direct after this six-week retrograde stint, you will be that much more ready to move quickly if you don't wallow in negative thinking. You will know you have a newfound freedom in Mars direct ready to assist you in making up for lost time. There will be no need to look back.

If your Sun sign is airy Gemini (May 20–June 20), a Mars retrograde can spin your curiosity in interesting directions. It is important not to get so spread out that you can't focus on any one thing for very long. You will need to exercise some willpower to finish what you start. But if you sense you are wasting all of your time and energy going in the wrong direction, give yourself the freedom to abort the mission. Your ability to look deeper into solving problems and doing research could intensify. Probing subjects of interest can be rewarding. Business instincts may become more spontaneous. This can be an inventive cycle that develops through exciting insights. Do exercise good judgment if you are attempting to make key job or business moves. Making solid decisions by showing patience is wise. Communicate with others clearly if you want to maintain closeness and harmony. Don't make hasty judgments. Be open to change because it might lead you to new opportunities.

If your Sun sign is airy Libra (September 22–October 22), you might be slower to make decisions during a Mars retrograde. This does not mean you are not mentally clear. It could have more to do with not being sure how others will react to your choices. There will be occasions during this retrograde when you might need to move forward anyway just to see if there really will be any resistance to the moves you need to make. It could be that you will need to remember to be more inclusive if you are making choices that will have a major impact on those you care about.

Be sure to be assertive if your own needs are not being met in your relationships. Being able to reach reasonable compromises during a Mars retrograde does alleviate much stress. Choose your battles wisely to avoid burning any bridges. Pull back from tension-provoking situations if that will help you maintain your emotional and mental balance. You could discover a surprising solution to an old issue during this Mars retrograde visit.

If your Sun sign is airy Aquarius (January 20–February 19), you may feel like it is taking twice as long to get things accomplished during a Mars retrograde. Mental exhaustion can occur if you don't rest your mind enough. "Rome was not built in a day" is something to remind yourself of daily while Mars is traveling backward. This cycle won't last forever, so be patient with yourself and others. It could appear that people are slower in responding to your needs. Try to remember they are walking through what may feel like cement during a Mars retrograde.

The world won't sit still during this retrograde time period as you proceed to conduct business and make decisions. Be sure to start ahead of time to meet any deadlines. You may think you have more time than you really do. You will experience less frustration with this cycle if you stay clear about your goals. Prioritizing what are the most important things you want to accomplish will give you a sense of order. Life could surprise you with new options you had not considered.

The Earth Signs (Taurus, Virgo, Capricorn) and Mars Retrograde

If your Sun sign is a member of the earth element, your determination to get goals accomplished efficiently could be tested more than you like by a Mars retrograde. You will need to reach back with some extra determination to work your way through obstacles. Life may seem like it is presenting you with icebergs to navigate around. That patience your element is known for will likely be needed to keep you from growing extremely frustrated while Mars is moving backward. This does not have to mean your life will move in reverse, though you may find yourself wondering if yesterday's actions really got you anywhere during a Mars retrograde. It could be that even when you are on top of your game, other people don't appear to have their own act together. Business affairs can be performed with the same precision you usually enjoy, but don't be surprised if even your best work has to be redone. It could be your timing was off or it was another person throwing a monkey wrench into your plans. This is fairly typical of a Mars retrograde. If you keep your expectations within reason, you will be much happier during this Mars visit. The passion you feel creatively or for life in general may not feel like it has that old familiar intensity. Don't worry. If you warm up slowly to whatever you are trying to accomplish, your energy will come through for you before you know it. It can take longer for your creative power to get activated during this cycle, but don't forget that you can be as successful exercising patience with yourself and others as you usually are.

If your Sun sign is earthy Taurus (April 19–May 20), a Mars retrograde could disturb the peaceful, easy feeling you cherish. Staying calm doing your everyday business might require you not to worry too much about the outcome of situations. In other words, you may need to step back and rethink a strategy that serves your purpose. Be flexible, because a Mars retrograde is one of those cycles that requires you to seek alternative solutions to ensure good results. Your sign is known for maintaining a steady sense of direction. Tweaking a plan will save you much aggravation. Making major changes during a Mars retrograde might not be the best decision if you can wait. It is the fear of change that can upset your nervous system, so try to stay centered no matter the challenges in front of you. Anger might surface from unresolved issues from the past. Don't feel you must respond to adversity impulsively. Time is a healer, and when Mars goes direct, it will likely be easier to resolve any disputes with others. You don't necessarily have to swallow your anger. Being assertive will help you get your needs met. Concentrating more on what you can control will put your mind into a more harmonious place.

If your Sun sign is earthy Virgo (August 22–September 22), a Mars retrograde will require some insight and a little patience on your part to get it working in your schedule. The usual meticulous way you like to proceed will get disrupted if you get into too big of a rush to get a job done. When handling business affairs, you may find you have to use your negotiation skills more than usual. Your work plate probably will fill up faster than you like. The key thing is not to panic. There likely is more time than you think to get what you need to accomplish tasks each day. Balancing work and leisure activities makes this Mars retrograde experience more pleasing. Don't try to make things perfect, as this will upset your nervous system and cause tension in your relationships. People might seem more demanding than usual, but don't let this bother you. Stay centered and communicate clearly what you need from others. This can be a very productive cycle for you if you stay organized and don't let the details grow too bothersome. Keep your mind focused on the big picture of what you are trying to accomplish each day. It will be your winning formula for a Mars retrograde.

If your Sun sign is earthy Capricorn (December 21–January 20), a Mars retrograde will test your stamina to finish what you start. This simply means you need to work smarter as well as harder. The key is taking the first step. Don't fear failing. Give yourself permission to make a mistake. If you practice being flexible, your goals and relationships will have a more positive feeling. Be sure to communicate with those closest to you. People may perceive you as too distant if you grow too secretive. Delays don't have to discourage you from giving your best effort. Your ambition drive may ebb and flow. Taking a short break from a plan might give you new insight into how to best achieve the right results. Maintain a positive outlook and life will reward you.

The Water Signs (Cancer, Scorpio, Pisces) and Mars Retrograde

If your Sun sign is a member of the water element, it may at times feel like your best energy is turning into steam during a Mars retrograde. If you stay calm and don't get overly anxious, before you know it your sense of direction will reclaim itself. Soon after a Mars retrograde begins, your mental and emotional energies could feel like they are working against each other. If you stay focused on your important daily goals, your life will move forward peacefully. When dealing with adversity or upsetting situations during a Mars retrograde, the key thing to remember is not to overreact. Sudden change might bother you during this cycle more than any other. Your creative power and self-confidence will be on the rise if you maintain a positive frame of mind. It is okay to take one step forward and three steps back during this time period, although your mind may not tell you this. It is a common occurrence to have your patience and mental strength tested during a Mars retrograde. You may notice other people feeling like they are in the same boat as you. Try not to take it too personally if your own life interests meet with some criticism. Your moods might fluctuate more than usual. This could be a signal that your passion to express your most cherished dreams is intensifying. Be true to yourself and don't ignore those you love. Self-awareness often is empowered during a Mars retrograde.

If your Sun sign is watery Cancer (June 22–July 22), a Mars retrograde can deepen your resolve to finish what you begin. The challenge is dealing with your moods. In some ways you may have to fool your mind if you have trouble getting a project started. This means to stop worrying by doing something you enjoy. You may find that adopting some new experiences will stimulate your motivation to stay focused. Your energy levels could go up and down on certain days during a Mars retrograde. Don't get discouraged. If you stay positive mentally, you will be much more productive during this cycle. Going back and completing unfinished projects can be accomplished. Resolving a relationship issue could give you a satisfied feeling. Your intuition is stronger when you communicate feelings. People will trust you more and give their strongest support if you talk openly. Healing old emotional wounds makes you internally stronger. Your creative instincts flourish if you believe in your ability.

If your Sun sign is watery Scorpio (October 22–November 21), a Mars retrograde might be somewhat easier for you to flow with than for some of the other signs. Why? This goes back to the fact that Mars is co-ruler of your sign, along with Pluto. So in other words you have a relationship with Mars energy built into your natural way of expressing yourself. This does not mean you will escape from all of the challenges a Mars retrograde can present to you. There might be a need to muster some extra courage to face obstacles in your path. There could be a tendency to grow timid when facing a sudden change you had not counted on. But don't worry. If you gather yourself—which might mean leaning on a friend or simply remaining calm—your problem-solving ability will surface. Be careful not to feel too responsible for the problems others create. Stay away from blaming someone else for a situation you put into play. Your negotiation skills will prove beneficial during a Mars retrograde. Don't underestimate your talent in marketing your skills. Abundance and good fortune depend on your willingness to seek harmony. Your goals get strengthened during a Mars retrograde, even if this does not seem that obvious. Patience will take you far, as will a steady determination to make a goal successful.

If your Sun sign is watery Pisces (February 19–March 20), a Mars retrograde can make you feel at times like you are treading water as you try to function on a day-to-day level. You don't need to let your worry get the best of you. Your bearings will likely get back on course shortly after you adjust to the energy of Mars retrograde. Your instincts on how to proceed forward can be interfered with by Mars moving backward. The interesting thing is your passion to make a dream come true empowers you during this cycle. Staying centered through your favorite ways of doing this makes this time period more enjoyable. Stay clear of trying to make something too perfect. It is okay if life gets messy. Be realistic in your expectations of yourself and others, as this is the best path you will find to make this a very productive Mars visit.

Surviving a Mars Retrograde Through Revitalizing Your Goals and Dreams

Mars Retrograde Survival Toolbox

- Channel your energy productively.
- Learn that patience is true wisdom.
- Be assertive rather than overly demanding.

• Express your ideas openly.

• Be aware of the needs of others.

Mars goes retrograde about every two years. A retrograde Mars time period lasts for about two months. How might this retrograde experience influence you? No matter your Sun sign, your energy level may not seem as vibrant as Mars begins to move backward through the sky. Don't take this too personally, as everyone in one way or another is probably experiencing this type of reaction. The speediness of Mars goes somewhat into a slowdown type of motion during its retrograde cycle. Try to imagine this as swimming against a strong current. It does not mean you won't arrive successfully at a targeted destination, but it may take a little more persistence to get the job done. It might even help to think of this as a test of your willpower.

Mars is a planet that normally symbolizes your need to act quickly on an idea. This is not exactly the same story when it is moving retrograde. You can still put your feet in motion forcefully, but it is not a bad idea to make sure before you leap that your reasoning is clear. There is a primitive instinct in everyone to make them think they can conquer the world, even when the odds may not exactly be in their favor. This is saying there might be an instance when you will go against your rational thinking to take on a challenge that later you will regret. This does not mean you have to abort an important heartfelt mission to get a plan accomplished. It is only saying that adopting a slower pace might open your eyes to more options. Make sure you are not letting raw emotion take over to such a degree that your mind is not perceiving a situation clearly. A Mars retrograde has the capacity to stir up feelings from the past that could interfere with your decisions in the present. Your memories of times past can suddenly resurface during a Mars retrograde. You could find yourself losing too much energy if you dwell on what you cannot change. Try to focus more on what you can do something about in the here and now. This will allow Mars to rev up your creative power during this retrograde, which will be a more satisfying feeling. Make sure you point this intense energy toward your goals. The enthusiasm you feel can bring a lot of success into your life. There is nothing like a Mars reboot of your sudden enthusiasm to let go of past difficulties and doubts to launch a sense of renewal.

When you read the Mars retrograde survival tips that follow, think of them as a guide to help you get better mileage out of this particular planetary movement. It is important to point out that a current Mars retrograde will not operate in your everyday life in exactly the same way as previous ones. What you hope to accomplish during one Mars retrograde may change drastically in a future one. What you needed from the past may or may not be the same in the current time period. The survival tips cover a wide range of issues.

Try to put the lessons that Mars has to offer you into favorable use for yourself. The survival tips are meant to empower you during this very challenging Mars retrograde. These two months need not frustrate you. You can use this time period as a source of newfound inner strength to more courageously pursue your hopes and dreams for a brighter future. Your identity can get stronger. A greater clarity about your need to be assertive might be discovered. Anger issues may be resolved. Your passion to find love and abundance can be rekindled. An uncompromising awareness to seek happiness and to share your vision with others can be stimulated by using the survival tips.

Tips for Surviving Mars Retrograde

Tip 1 for Surviving Mars Retrograde: Don't Burn Your Bridges

A Mars retrograde is supposed to slow you down, but this is not always the case. Mars can push you to move through your life with amazing speed. There is a drive offered by this planet to blast your way through any obstacle in front of you. Forward movement is more the natural tendency inspired by this planet, rather than retracing your steps of yesterday. Mars can sometimes influence you to think the past never existed. This planet has an unusual capacity to arouse an instinct to erase the past more quickly, especially during this type of Mars cycle.

Retrogrades push everyone to look back at their life to some extent. This action planet may trigger your brain into thinking you need to rid yourself of a current situation in a hurry. Flying away to what seems like freedom from the past becomes a top priority. You might even find that you lose sleep until you rid yourself of what you think of as an impediment to your peace of mind. Your impulse control to think rationally is being bypassed by a sense of urgency to move into new life circumstances. When you are mentally clear, this tendency will not be as prevalent and you will be more likely to get positive results.

If you are letting fear or turning away from conflict be the deciding factor, you may go from the frying pan into what will seem like a fire or a worse experience. So during a Mars retrograde try to slow time down just enough to let your best mental faculties weigh into your decisions. You will be glad you did at a later time when Mars turns direct. You will likely look back and wonder what you were thinking if you did act with reckless abandonment.

Acting on a sudden opportunity may be your ticket to a better future. Just be sure you don't haphazardly let go of people or jobs that may not be as bad as you think. Hasty judgments might come back to bite you at a later date. You might still be able to correct bad decisions lacking forethought, but much time and energy could be expended to fix impulsive moves you made that possibly could have been avoided with a little more patience. Smoother transitions from one move to the next give you a more harmonious feeling. Sometimes others need you to clearly indicate what you need from them to keep each of you happy. There could be better ways to leave situations just in case you need those resources later.

During a Mars retrograde it is wise to remember that a fog can cloud your thinking, so be sure to act with insight. There is always the chance you may want to reenter a past place of work or revisit a past friendship. Maintaining contact with the past might serve a useful purpose you are not presently perceiving. You don't need to look backward as you step forward. This is just saying not to undervalue the people and experiences you are now having. They may even be key building blocks for an abundant future. Watch out for reacting too hastily. Rashness could cause you to waste valuable resources. Mars is a great planet to ride bravely toward new horizons. The trick is to make sure you don't leave behind what you might need later. There is a powerful me-focus in Mars that is wonderful in making sure your own needs are met.

Under a Mars retrograde, there is the possibility that taking quick action could cause you to miss seeing the whole picture. Important details may be out of your immediate line of sight. There is the possibility you could be in denial about what is good concerning a current situation. Focusing only on what you see as bad about present circumstances gets in the way of moving forward. If you are running away from the past, you will likely have to confront what you are leaving all over again somewhere down the road. If leaving a situation is what you need to find greater happiness and abundance, then by all means go forth confidently.

Tip 2 for Surviving Mars Retrograde: Channel Your Anger with Clarity

Staying in touch with expressing anger is important during a Mars retrograde. Channeling this raw emotional intensity clearly can be a real challenge during the retrograde cycle of Mars. Why? The retrograde version of Mars tends to push your energy inward. This does not mean you can't be very assertive as needed. It is only saying that the usual way of letting anger out has a greater tendency to be more unpredictable. It has a way of being hidden during this retrograde, unlike in any other planetary retrograde time period. Sometimes anger builds to a boiling point if you don't let it out and can erupt like a volcano.

This has a greater possibility of occurring during a Mars retrograde because the tendency to hold it back is stronger at this time. This does not mean every Mars retrograde will cause this to occur, but there is always one that will make this a reality to encounter. You will get stronger in tuning in to this energy, as it is capable of empowering you. Your life stays in harmony with clear expressions of anger.

Anger is more likely to get scattered in ways you had not counted on during Mars retrograde. What comes out of your mouth may not be what your mind intended to say. It is as though your thinking and your favorite forms of communicating your thoughts don't appear to be in sync. This might even shock you when it occurs and feel like it is out of your control. Emotional confusion is not so unusual during angry episodes.

Anger can even get diluted or weakened during this particular planet's retrograde motion. You could be practicing what you are going to say to someone regarding a situation. The dress rehearsal to prepare for your confrontation goes wonderfully. When it is time to go on stage and put your anger right out there to be seen, suddenly you start to realize your intensity to say what has been on your mind has leaked out. Where did it go? Perhaps you held on to the anger for too long, or it might be you are no longer really that mad after all. It could be that your emotions are watering down your anger to such a point that you are not feeling it as strongly when you go to let it out at a person or situation. Time is an interesting thing to consider when it comes to anger. Sometimes it is the healer that helps you rid yourself of it if you have been holding on to it for too long. Perhaps it has been eating away at your health and sense of well-being for far too long. As days go by, you may have found an inner way to resolve your anger. This happens more often than you might think.

There are no rigid rules regarding when and how to express anger. There will be occasions during a Mars retrograde when you will be thankful you did hesitate in being angry at a person. You may gain insight into how to deal with an issue better. If you truly need to let someone know how displeased you are with their behavior, then sooner is better than later in expressing your angry feelings to them. If you hold on to anger for too long, it can come out in ways you did not plan on. This is not good for you or those around you.

You probably have heard of passive-aggressive behavior. This is a technique often used by individuals who disguise their anger by trying to manipulate you. They are likely trying to sabotage your attempt to be happy and successful. If you are trying to deal with a person who is using anger to control your thoughts and actions, it is especially troublesome during a Mars retrograde. During this planet's retrograde movement, it could be harder to decipher if you are falling victim to this trickery. It is because Mars moving retrograde is easier to make more invisible whatever someone's motivation might be to fool you. Make sure you are not the person hiding your anger to the point of being the manipulator. In the end, it works against you to express anger in this manner. If you sense someone is steering you purposely in wrong directions through a misuse of their own anger, you either need to call the person's bluff or just stay away from them. Sometimes distancing yourself will be the only wise policy made available to you.

When someone is trying to hide their true motivations for purposely desiring to get the best of you, it is definitely not Mars being used in its most productive way. It is actually better if you and the other person get your differences out in the open, even if the communication gets somewhat heated. Sometimes you have to clear the air, as the old saying goes, to bring the temperature down to a cooler degree. Then you both may be able to hear what you really need to resolve a problem.

Mars is constantly coaxing you to be direct in making your ideas known. Even more important to keep in mind is that Mars represents a primordial instinct to act on impulse. Anger is very much a spontaneous outburst of how you feel. If it has been building up for a long time, it can be released with what seems like an uncontrollable force. Anger resembles a hurricane-like wind of force, and if not pointed in the right direction, it may be self-destructive or ruin your harmony. Then again, when you discharge this energy, it can feel good or even therapeutic. The key is being conscious about who or what you really are angry at during a Mars retrograde. You will waste much less time and your vitality will stay strong if you are really clear about what you are feeling. Anger is very connected to your creative power, so you will be much more successful in the world if you are in touch with your most intense emotions.

In the world of business, sparring a bit with others is par for the course. If you need to be competitive or even bordering on aggressive, you are likely to find acceptance. The energy that fuels anger often is better placed in the work arena.

Physical exercise and sexual release are other great methods to keep your anger calmer. If you like to meditate or take relaxing walks, it helps balance anger. There will be those occasions during a Mars retrograde when honest communication will take the high voltage out of potentially explosive exchanges. This is a tried-and-true formula that seems to often work in your favor.

What are the major benefits of being in touch with your anger during a Mars retrograde? You will have greater self-confidence. Putting your best foot forward to show you believe in your abilities actually gains momentum when you know how to release anger appropriately. It is reflected in your body language. A Mars retrograde will influence you to pull your anger back and hold it, like stretching a rubber band without breaking it. It is the focusing power of anger that can steady your creative flow. Another way to think of this is that the same energy that fills you with anger when aimed at your goals fires them up with great vitality. This is not saying anger is a bad thing. It is only making the point that having a balanced sense of using anger promotes the abundance you seek in your life. Your relationships benefit as well when you get a handle on anger. Passion and love result when you are making the right use of anger.

Tip 3 for Surviving Mars Retrograde:
Get Enough Rest

Mars is the high-energy drink of life. It is natural caffeine. This planet sparks your endorphin levels to their maximum peak. If you are constantly pushing the limits during a Mars retrograde, your physical strength can begin to lessen suddenly without any warning. Perhaps it is the universe's message for you to give your body some rest. The old saying "Rome was not built in a day" is good to remember. A retrograde usually will naturally entice you to reflect before taking action. This is not always true of a Mars retrograde. The tremendous forceful push to move forward is often present in this planet's influence even during its retrograde cycle. Forgetting to slow down actually occurs often during a Mars retrograde. In the haste to get things done, your mind can get trapped in a constant race to get to the finish line. So knowing when to stop is good for your well-being.

Getting enough sleep is sometimes a challenge during a Mars retrograde. As you are trying to fall asleep, you don't want to keep thinking about what you need to do the next day. Equally as troublesome is dwelling on what you did not finish during the present day. Setting boundaries in your schedule for when to stop working might be needed. Insomnia is a potential Mars theme. Each person has their own favorite ways to enter a sleep state. It could be reading a book, meditating, listening to sounds that calm you, taking a prescribed medication that lulls you to sleep, or another technique. The main message is to get the amount of sleep you need to maintain your health. Sleep deprivation eventually makes you less effective in achieving your goals. You will get to a higher production level with rest and will even feel happier.

If you have a very active life, you may need to start your downtime earlier in the evening, especially during a Mars retrograde. Your body and mind could require more rest during some Mars retrograde time periods. Brain stimulation is linked to Mars, because in astrology this planet rules the head. Whatever you can do to slow your mental activity before trying to go to sleep is a good idea. Have you ever heard of a power nap? It was invented to counteract the Mars impact and to reinvigorate our energy levels. If you need a short sleep break of even fifteen to twenty minutes, it could increase your creative power immensely. Try it. You might like it.

Burnout results during Mars retrogrades when rushing from one project to the next. The wonderful thing about Mars is that it gives you that get-up-and-go to initiate action. It does require a bit of discipline to hit the brakes as needed. So drive with wisdom this fiery planet with a revved-up engine that can get your mind to go from zero to sixty in the blink of an eye.

There is another important dimension to dealing with a Mars retrograde when it comes to getting enough rest. If you are totally bored, you are going to find it difficult to settle into a peaceful state of mind. Mars is a restless planet constantly pulsating with a certain degree of excitement as it runs through your mental reasoning ability. This is supposed to arouse your interest in keeping your mind occupied with whatever you enjoy doing. It is a delicate balance between being mentally active and growing lethargic. Finding that harmonious meeting place of pushing to accomplish goals and pausing for rest is required. With practice, you can get good at this. It is a good thing to do during a Mars retrograde, as it ensures positive health results.

If you get some exercise, you are probably going to find a better flow with a Mars retrograde. Your stress levels will be easier to manage with physical activity. Mars gives you that extra adrenaline to seize the opportunities and meet the challenges of any day. Pacing yourself and taking good care of your body will go far in helping you get the most out of a Mars retrograde.

Tip 4 for Surviving Mars Retrograde: Defend Your Territorial Rights

Mars is not called the warrior planet for no reason. This planet shows us how to be strong in claiming our turf. If someone is trying to interfere with your right to be yourself, Mars energy is what you need to fight off the obstruction. The competitive spirit offered by Mars has no rival among the other planets. There might be a Mars retrograde where you find your assertiveness to be not as strong as when the planet is moving direct. Don't let this bother you. It could be you are in a new relationship or trying to defend your ideas with others. You may be wondering what happened to your feistiness.

There is a strong self-focus that is ordinarily part of the Mars package deal. If you are feeling overwhelmed by someone else's demands on your time, money, or space, you will have to put your foot down at times. It is very possible that you might be surprised how fast you can tune in to the fighting spirit of Mars. Mars does play off of your emotions. When you start to really feel you must respond to the challenge presented by a situation, your Mars expression might suddenly burst onto the scene. This can occur so spontaneously that you might not even know when you suddenly became so brave.

Mars has a strong link to identity, or our self-image. If you allow others to push you around too much, you are not going to feel on top of your own game. You don't need to become warlike but might need to bark loudly. If you hide your own needs too much, your life will get out of balance. Mars retrograde can work to your advantage if even at first glance this does not seem to be happening. How do you do this? It could be that when you get some physical space from someone who is intimidating you, it could allow you to be more direct with the person. There are occasions when getting away from a person's negative impact on you allows for your own response to build more clearly. Think of it as taking a timeout from the situation to regain your clarity and strength to deal with a problem. You need the space to stop having your own energy robbed by a person trying to overwhelm you. You have to tune in to your sense of personal empowerment to claim the territory you are entitled to.

If a new challenge has you feeling uncomfortable, you will need to be patient. Entering new situations during a Mars retrograde or not long before one has begun may mean it will take you a week or two to find your footing. Warming up to confronting obstacles, whether in the form of a person or a life circumstance, might require some input from a friend. In the end, you will be the one pushing for what you need.

Talking to others you trust about a challenge could give you the insight and confidence to deal with an obstacle. Mars inspires courage. The trick is not to let fear dominate you. Mars moving backward might cause a delay in standing up for your rights. If you stay persistent, you can turn a negative situation into a positive one. The lessons learned during a Mars retrograde about believing in your ability to fight for what is right are worth any struggle.

Tip 5 for Surviving Mars Retrograde: Finish What You Start

The initiating force of Mars is very similar to the power of jet propulsion. It is one of the great wonders of the world. Mars helping you close the deal during its retrograde movement can be another story. Why might this be? You may start to question if you are on the right path to the finish line about halfway there. If this does occur, don't feel singled out. There are a lot of people likely going through the same experience. Mars produces an inner restlessness to conquer new frontiers well before current commitments are completed. The trick is to keep one foot in the present even if your other foot is tempted to blast off in a new direction. You can live in both worlds successfully. You don't have to give up on a pull to the future but might need to put a goal on the back burner so you will finish what you set out to do.

There are times during this retrograde cycle when you will need to take a new assessment of your progress toward a goal. You might even figure out a better method of getting something accomplished, saving you time, money, and stress. Digging up the seed before getting a job done is when you get into trouble. The frustration is no fun. You will need to trust your instincts that you are proceeding correctly or at least give your ideas a fair chance to succeed. Don't let self-doubt talk you out of giving an idea enough time to come to fruition. Otherwise you won't really know if you are moving in the right direction.

Mars stimulates impulsive action. This planet is great for putting out a fire with great speed. This calls for an urge to get something done fast. Your mind might get into a hit-and-run frenzy in an extreme way under a Mars retrograde. This means you will start and stop repeatedly and not get done what is required. The great physicist Einstein said that insanity was doing the same thing over and over again and expecting a different result. So if you find yourself obsessing over something with no reward, the best thing to do is to stop. Getting refocused is the best plan. You may need to distract yourself away from a major plan to give your mind a break. Why? Because your opportunity to gain new insight has a better chance to be discovered. There is a fine line between forcing the outcome of a situation and taking a more relaxed approach. You might need to accept that during a Mars retrograde there will be days that feel like you are taking a step forward and other days that seem like two steps back—but the next day could find you moving three steps forward. It might be slower progress, but your determination will be rewarded if you don't give up too easily. Your patience will get tested, but perhaps the old saying "no pain, no gain" applies here. Reasonable persistence is something to keep in mind.

Tip 6 for Surviving Mars Retrograde: Share Center Stage

Wanting to make your ideas visible is a Mars theme. Getting the recognition you desire and feel like you deserve is pushed by Mars energy. If people are not listening, it does not make you feel accepted. During a Mars retrograde there can be a heightened sensitivity if you are coming to the realization others are not paying enough attention to your needs. It is not that you may be wanting to steal someone else's thunder. It is that strong desire to have your opinions recognized that might intensify during this retrograde cycle. If you give in to being ignored, you probably will feel miserable. The natural inclination you will tune in to when experiencing the full brunt of Mars energy is to make a path for yourself no matter the obstacles.

Mars will fire up that passion to make others hear you. You might even want to scream to get a reaction from others. There are various reasons people may not be giving you the attention you deserve. One is that someone's insecurities could be making them uncomfortable with your own opinions. They feel threatened even though you are not intending for this to happen. It can be easier to step on someone's toes during a Mars retrograde. Why? Because you may not be aware you are doing this. You may be so caught up in your own enthusiasm that you lose sight of those around you. You can unintentionally cause hurtful feelings.

Try to remember that the retrograde movement of this planet can set off reactions unexpectedly, like a match to gasoline. You may be shocking someone just as much as would happen if Mars were moving direct. People's reaction times can be slower during a Mars retrograde, but there are certain retrogrades of the angry red celestial wanderer that might find a person reacting more emotionally to your actions. So try to be conscious of this, as it could make a big difference in maintaining the peace and cooperation you see with others.

Perhaps you are challenging a person's authority or expertise, making them feel uncomfortable. This can cause a person to prefer that you remain invisible. In this instance, someone is trying to throw you off the stage. Another explanation for others dodging your ideas is that someone is jealous of you but might be hiding this from you. Someone may not want you performing with them and may want to push you out of their path. Mars retrogrades can put you in circumstances that challenge your willpower to make your ideas known. After all, Mars is the star of combat throughout history. When you are exhibiting a warrior strength in pursuing your dreams, someone may feel threatened or simply not understand you. The sharing of power can be a real problem during a Mars retrograde.

If you demand all of the attention, it produces tension in your relationships. A Mars retrograde can sometimes make it difficult to be aware of when you are wanting to get your own way too much of the time. Finding your objective awareness is essential to sharing the spotlight with others. The give and take of attention during a Mars retrograde is essential to find harmony in your social interactions. You don't want to always give in to the likes and dislikes of another person.

If you don't expect others to always agree with you, a Mars retrograde is more flowing. You don't really need the applause from others to move toward fulfilling your hopes and dreams, although it never hurts to remind those closest to you that you need their support once in a while. After all, they will be asking this of you. It makes sharing the spotlight that much easier. There is enough room for both of you to feel important. You don't want to lose sight of this even if you need to place a reminder on your refrigerator.

Tip 7 for Surviving Mars Retrograde: Learn to Forgive

You can bring emotional baggage into a Mars retrograde that gets stirred up like it is in a blender, creating confusion. There may be unresolved anger at someone or even yourself that brings you into a negative state of mind. You may not have had a clue you were carrying such a load of hidden anger from the past. Letting go of past differences with people is no easy assignment. It takes a certain amount of willpower and a change in attitude to release bad feelings about others.

You will find that your creative energy will increase if you are able to forgive someone who may have betrayed your trust. It might be hard to convince yourself that releasing old anger is liberating, but it is true. Holding on to old bad energy has a way of eating into your mental and physical well-being. This does not mean you have to completely forget what someone may have done to anger or disappointment you. You may still have to distance yourself from a person if you really can't make peace with them. But in the end, you are better off ridding yourself of past negativity.

If you find a path to forgiveness, you will not have to keep the energy of these memories locked up inside of you. Your intuition will benefit and lead you to greener pastures where you may find the harmony you seek. The energy you lose when you do not forgive others could be put toward more productive outlets. Maybe it is better said that you want to release bad memories or feelings so they don't rule you. It will be a wonderful experience to use a Mars retrograde to transcend what is no longer serving any fruitful purpose in your life.

Forgiving yourself is even more difficult sometimes. You may want to read the previous sentence over again because you don't want to forget it! A Mars retrograde is actually one of the better cycles to accomplish this feat. When moving backward, Mars has a lot of healing energy to fix old wounds. It has a unique way of surgically removing old scar tissue from previous emotional wounds. You may be angry at yourself for something you caused to occur. Sooner or later you will need to let yourself off the hook. Focusing on your mistakes won't make you feel any better. This is not the best way to move in a new direction.

Perhaps you do need to learn something from a mistake you made. Use Mars retrograde to get clear about owning up to a behavior. You may need to ask someone to forgive you. The main message here is not to dwell on what you did wrong. Learn from the past, as it is a great teacher. Use this cycle to gain new insight and a renewed sense of self. You will find empowerment when you make an honest assessment of your actions. Forgiveness is a powerful tool. It opens the door to fresh new insights and could ignite new opportunities. Let it light the way to new growth. There might be a rebirth awaiting you that is a pleasant surprise.

Tip 8 for Surviving Mars Retrograde:
Take That Leap of Faith

You may find yourself in a Mars retrograde that requires you to trust your instincts if an opportunity presents itself that is too good to let go by. Even though a Mars retrograde cycle more often than not is sending you a message to be cautious, you may need to grab a good offer that is on the table. Making changes during one of these retrograde time periods can be stressful, but you may feel up to the challenge. Sometimes you might need a push from a friend or family member to encourage you to take an adventurous jump forward. If you do make a significant change while Mars is temporarily moving backward through the sky, then don't look back. It is important to proceed full steam ahead. When Mars moves direct again, you won't have to worry as much about whether you made the right decision. The direct thrust of this fiery planet will put your worries to rest, or at least it should.

It is not out of the ordinary to take a risk during a Mars retrograde. Playing it safe is not really the Mars method of enticing you to be decisive. This planet may suddenly show you how to tap into a newfound courage. Your fear of change may relax in the presence of a feisty self-confidence brought to you during this retrograde. This planet has a way of stimulating the part of your mind that is spontaneous.

Whether you usually operate on impulse or are more of the type who likes to look before leaping, Mars can pull you along even if you are screaming not to go so fast. This fireball of a planet will tug on you to let go of the past and seek a brighter future. Mars would just as soon you bypass your overly thoughtful tendencies and throw caution to the wind. After all, in many ways it is the job of Mars to pry you loose from comfort zones so you can have new experiences. So you might need to fasten your seatbelt and let this planet drive you into new frontiers with vaster highways to abundance.

If you doubt your ability to handle a new situation, Mars retrograde could instill the confidence you need. The trick is to take that first step to meet Mars halfway. The power of your own intention is what is required. You may find an empowerment by forming the thought patterns needed to confront your own fear of making a change. The positive vision you put out to the universe could be just what you need to be successful. Breaking through your resistance to having a better future may not be as difficult as it appeared. After you transition into new circumstances, you likely will be pleasantly surprised by the creative energy it releases.

Tip 9 for Surviving Mars Retrograde: Don't Be Working Just to Be Working

It is possible during a Mars retrograde to forget to stop working. It is the passion to keep pushing yourself beyond your limits that may be the reason for this occurring. Or the driving force behind this behavior might be the anxiety you feel because you think you may be missing out on getting something done on time. Don't feel bad. This is a common occurrence during Mars retrograde. You could be one of those people who are addicted to always desiring to have a project in front of you. If it gets too obsessive, you will find yourself repeating actions over and over again that are unnecessary. Mars is a restless planet and is happy to share this squirmy type of trait with you.

During a Mars retrograde, there might come a time when you need to separate yourself from a tendency to be driven to always be doing something. You may be a person who feels guilty when resting. It is great to have goals. Just remember to know your limits. If you feel great anxiety when not working, it is a pattern worth changing. It will take some persistent practice to turn your mind away from work. Cultivating other interests is one of the best ways to find the balance you need. You may even feel like you are going through withdrawal symptoms, as if you are discarding a bad habit. Not realizing you can't live without constantly working is part of the issue. Your mind and body will thank you for hopping off a merry-go-round of constant action. It may bring a sense of relief you did not know would feel so good.

Setting some boundaries will help you from exhausting yourself needlessly. There are possibly going to be certain days when you will have to put in some extra time and effort to get a job done. Knowing when to stop takes practice. It may help to have a friend or family member tell you when it is time to quit. Occasionally it helps to have an outside objective observer keep an eye on us to make sure we don't go overboard in the work world. So don't get too defensive if someone who knows you well suggests toning down your work just a bit.

A Mars retrograde is actually a wonderful time to get off the treadmill of always putting yourself to work. It is a great thing to be needed by others. Also, it is good to want to make others happy with the work you do for them. Be sure to be aware if you are trying too hard to get others to admire you. A trap during a Mars retrograde is feeling like there is something to prove to others. This may be a reason to keep pushing yourself way past what is needed. Keep your expectations reasonable and you will be much happier.

Tip 10 for Surviving Mars Retrograde: Take Care of Business

Mars provides plenty of enthusiasm and drive to be successful in business goals. When you ride the adventurous waves of this planet courageously, there is no real limit to what you might be able to accomplish. Mars fires up your enterprising instincts like no other planet can do. The next sentence might sound like a contradiction to the previous three sentences. A Mars retrograde presents a dilemma in that it asks you to be sure of the actions you take before putting them into motion. It is not saying to put your hopes and dreams on hold, but only to try to determine ahead of time if your heartfelt motivations will get you to your desired destination.

You may have planned an event or job interview before Mars turned retrograde. That is fine. Just be aware that the intensity that was there when you made your first approach for a scheduled activity may seem to have lessened when it comes time to engage in the event. Don't worry, because the same excitement can be activated once again. Sometimes it is the anxiety that appears during a Mars retrograde that interferes with your self-confidence. If you stay centered and calm, that same gusto can reappear with the same force.

Your negotiating strength can be empowered during a Mars retrograde. Be as prepared as possible when entering a deal. Try to stay cognizant of someone else's needs during a transaction. You will find that your suggestions and ideas will be that much better received by others if you show you are hearing their point of view.

If you are making a large purchase during a Mars retrograde, take it slow. Be open to insights from those you trust. This is a time period when getting a little help from your friends in terms of offering an impartial opinion could help you avoid making big mistakes. Don't commit to a contract that does not feel just right. It might be a Mars retrograde that is coaxing you to wait for its direct motion. Why? Because it may be that at that time your mind will be clearer and more decisive.

Patience can be difficult to locate during a Mars retrograde. You may want something so bad that you don't want to wait. There is a fine line between being too patient and trusting that impulse to take a risk. Giving yourself permission to put a plan into motion may be what you must do in order to take a well-calculated gamble. Just be sure you can afford to lose what you venture.

There is always the chance that during a Mars retrograde your best laid-out schedule will get thwarted by circumstances beyond your control. Try not to get too upset with yourself or others. This is simply part of making peace with a Mars retrograde. The better you get at adjusting to a sudden change, the more you will find that taking care of business won't be that difficult.

Tip 11 for Surviving Mars Retrograde: Maintain Your Passion

A Mars retrograde can sometimes interfere with your sex drive. Don't be alarmed. The reason for this is you could have bad timing with a partner. One or both of you may have schedules that are in overdrive. Fatigue might be a problem. Exhaustion does not increase a person's desire for sex. It can bring passion to a fast halt. Mars retrograde could be adding extra stress over worrying about unfinished projects. Being distracted by life's everyday demands may put you and a lover at odds as to when is the best time for sex. Putting each other first may need to become a top priority.

Perhaps it is true that the demands on your time are great. Life in the fast lane is not so uncommon in modern life. Making time for each other is likely going to be an issue. If you are already in an existing relationship, it might help to have a regular date night just for yourselves. Making a commitment to finding quality time for being with someone is one way to improve your sex life. Catching up with each other's hopes and dreams is another perk for creating a safe-haven time together. The two months of a Mars retrograde may seem like an eternity if your sex drive is in reverse. Your intentions could be good but the results frustrating. Be patient and think of creative ways to keep the romantic fires lit. If you need to break up the routines to add some spark, then go for it. Remember that Mars is a planet that emphasizes adventure. Spontaneity could be the road map to your own heart and that of a partner. It never hurts to surprise someone with something unexpected that puts both of you in the right mood to make love. Part of foreplay is preparing the right sexual atmosphere.

If it is anger at each other that is interfering with your lovemaking, then you have to address this. Anger and passion actually travel along the same mental circuits. Old anger issues can block the expression of love and especially wanting to have sex with someone. A Mars retrograde is an opportunity to talk about what is causing the anger so you can get back to having pleasurable sex.

Exercise is one way to bring your passion back from the dead. There are some Mars retrogrades that put your energy to sleep. If you feel too passive, then working out is a method to fire up passion. If you lack energy, it is hard to feel very excited about love or any of your main goals. To get into sync with Mars, you need to take action. Get into motion. Move. Taking that first step to go on a walk or run might be just what you need to get back on the passion track. If you are feeling down over a disappointing experience, your zest for life might seem like it is in a downward spiral. Getting more exercise can bring back your desire for sex and increase your overall energy levels.

Your moods could be all over the map. Little things can be more bothersome than usual when Mars is moving backward. Tuning in to your emotions is easier if you talk them out. You might be surprised at how your desire to be sexy and to feel more alive awakens when you reveal your feelings.

Tip 12 for Surviving Mars Retrograde:
Initiate New Stimulating Experiences

Mars inspires you to courageously begin new adventures. There is a push from this planet that can be very forceful. A Mars retrograde has the possibility of getting you to question a new experience shortly after it begins. It is important at this point to be sure to take your time before making a final decision about whether you made the right choice. There is a warming-up period that occurs during a Mars retrograde particularly if you have begun a new venture. Finding that objectivity is the key to the success of whatever new direction you have embarked upon. Walking in new directions can fill you with a sense of renewal.

A new romance may begin with a strong physical attraction and great passion. This is not unusual. As the romantic intensity begins to settle, you may start wondering how far you want to proceed with the relationship. Eventually you will want to know just how compatible you may be with someone for a longer relationship. A Mars retrograde might find you denying what you really need from a person. You may be wanting to know what it is you can expect from this person in the future.

Communication is the answer to getting an early clue about whether you are in a relationship that will bring you the happiness you seek. Don't be afraid to ask questions that will give you a better idea of what you feel you really need to know about a partner. Sooner or later you will want to know what someone expects from you. A Mars retrograde has a tendency to stimulate an inquisitive nature in you about why someone wants to be involved with you. Neither of you likely will get all of your questions answered during a Mars retrograde. Not getting really deep too fast may be something to remember during this cycle. Enjoying the dating part of a relationship flows better with a Mars retrograde. Finding out some things you have in common is often promoted by a Mars retrograde.

A new job might be exciting and generate some anxiety at the same time. Be patient with yourself in learning what is required when starting a new work situation. Mars retrograde is a good time to impress others with your willingness to work hard. You may put too much pressure on yourself to get a job done faster. Believing in your ability will have a calming effect and go far in helping you become a success.

Taking those first steps into new experiences sometimes is scary. You might fear failure. This occurs with greater frequency during a Mars retrograde. Don't be timid in testing the waters of a new endeavor. You likely are stronger than you realize. One good thing to remember about Mars is that once you put an idea into motion, good things can follow. Your self-confidence will be contagious if you truly believe in a plan.

During a Mars retrograde, any new endeavors will require having patience with yourself and others. This includes moving into a new home or becoming a parent for the first time. Perhaps you are starting college or opening a new business. All life events that begin during a Mars retrograde bring on greater stress. This is not such a bad thing. It is in initiating new experiences that you find great growth and the vigor to find happiness.

Tip 13 for Surviving Mars Retrograde:
Renew Your Identity

A major theme of Mars is identity. It is a planet that stimulates "who am I?" questions and does this frequently during a retrograde. This is not something to be worried about. Think of this as getting to know yourself on a deeper level. This is a process that is really attempting to make you internally stronger. There is a payoff in your external world, and you can also move forward with greater clarity.

Reinventing yourself could cross your mind during a Mars retrograde. This does not mean you need to change everything about yourself. Your willpower to create a new reality might become more of a priority. You may choose not to act on these thoughts during the retrograde. It may be more a matter of envisioning what a different you would be like. Just imagining a new life could fill you with greater energy.

If you fear being judged for making empowering decisions, that is not so unusual. First you have to work through an inner resistance to moving into a world that better matches who you are in the present. You might not need to leave your entire current life behind. There may only need to be a minor change. Then again, if you truly require a total makeover, this Mars retrograde could be a dress rehearsal for the real thing. Courage sometimes does not come until you take that first step on the path to a new horizon. The universe will greet your intention to become a renewed you with open arms if you take that first fiery step forward that Mars can invigorate. You might be surprised and relieved how simple making a change is after you do it.

Sometimes the universe seems to purposely shake us up when we over-identify with a particular side of ourselves. Perhaps you are too attached to your appearance and too preoccupied with being accepted for the way you look. It is okay if you really feel you need to update your wardrobe or change your hairstyle. Just make sure you are doing it more for yourself than just to make someone else happy.

During a Mars retrograde, there is a chance you may feel a need to find a job or pursue a business that better matches your identity. You may be hoping to find the right fit for yourself. You may get the idea that you have outgrown the work you have been doing. A new challenge energizes your mind. After all, Mars brings out the spirit of adventure in everyone. So walking in a new career direction is not so unusual. It may be a hobby you explore that rounds out your sense of self. It is easy to get bored during a Mars retrograde. Adding a little excitement in the form of new experiences may be just what you need.

There is always the possibility of tweaking your self-image during a Mars retrograde. Perhaps you want to be perceived as more self-confident. A new boldness may become part of your personality. Your persona, or the mask you show to others, could seem brighter. Developing a more positive attitude can attract successful outcomes. Looking like you have a well-conceived plan convinces people to believe in you. Selling ideas has greater influence if your face and body language reflects decisiveness.

What if your usual way of getting what you want is too aggressive? Part of forming a new identity is learning not to be too forceful in getting your needs met. Sharing your power takes some trust. Giving others a chance to voice their own opinions and to show their own strength openly solidifies your relationships. This is another way your identity can transform. Negotiating to create harmony with someone has a payoff. Your own inner fortitude benefits in knowing you have people in your life who are strong allies.

Mars retrograde might be a time to get to know yourself on a deeper level. If you are usually a fast-moving and very outgoing person, then this cycle may get you to look in the mirror. Mars retrograde may tune you in to ways to slow down. Reexamining your actions as a process to get clearer about your inner motivations for making choices is not so unusual during a Mars retrograde. Your identity and self-confidence are stronger when you are not afraid to tune in to your feelings.

Revealing your inner world to a trusted friend may be a gateway to a sense of renewal. Your energy to explore what makes you happy gets stimulated through letting others see your true self. If there are issues about yourself or habits you want to change, this retrograde could be the time to get it done. It might be a minor adjustment you would like to make. There might be a behavior that interferes with your way of getting close to people. Self-honesty can be transforming and empowering. A Mars retrograde has the capacity to reveal to you the way to turn past negative thoughts and actions into positive expressions. The key is being willing to change.

Tip 14 for Surviving Mars Retrograde:
Repair Broken Partnerships

A Mars retrograde may find you going back and attempting to fix relationships disrupted by strong disagreements. Perhaps you decided to end a partnership or friendship and now realize you need this person. Yes, sometimes this happens unexpectedly during a Mars retrograde. You may be wanting to do business with someone once again but are not sure if they will be receptive. If you are clear about the source of your previous troubles with a person, it helps greatly in putting the alliance back together in one piece. There are more than likely going to be some compromises needed to make the connection work smoothly the way you need it to. You don't need to give away the whole farm, as the old saying goes, but you probably will need to bend a little. You will need to really think this through before approaching a new agreement.

Mars is not exactly the most objective energy. This fiery red planet often puts your mind into rapid machine gunfire in what seems like a split second. You can go from a calm feeling of serenity into an emotional explosion when this planet stimulates your thinking. It is important to bear in mind the strong self-interest motivated by this planet, and it can even intensify during its retrograde movement. This means it is okay to have your own needs in mind, but the other person will have their own agenda as well. With patience, you can avoid pushing only for your own plan. This is one of the things that can work in your favor if you slow down long enough to let your most rational thinking take the lead. This retrograde cycle has the capacity to stimulate the insight to work for a win-win strategy.

Exchanging ideas with someone will get heated quickly if old issues start to resurface. If you can stay away from blaming each other for past clashes, you will get much further in getting back to doing business together again in an amicable way. What you are really aiming for is a mutually beneficial arrangement. If you and another person sense getting together again is empowering each of you, then you have a winning formula. What is broken between you has a much better chance of being fixed if you keep fairness in play.

Romantic relationships can be healed during a Mars retrograde as well, although they are more challenging due to the potential for past problems to rear their heads again. If there was once a feeling of love and passion between you, then it can be rekindled during a Mars retrograde. Try not to force getting back together faster than it can realistically occur. This is easier said than done. If you are feeling insecure, trying to rush a sense of togetherness will backfire in ways you won't like. You may need time to warm up to the closeness again just as much as your partner will require this. Respect each other's space.

Usually trust issues are at the heart of erasing past differences. Going slower need not scare you. It is a good sign under a Mars retrograde to let time be a healer. Try not to forget that this is a healing process and might work in ways that will surprise you. You and the other person will gradually come closer as the trust builds between you. Letting go of past anger at one another helps. Old negative behavior patterns displayed by each of you need to be left behind. It is only going to work if a new start seems real to each of you. A key ingredient for success is making a pact not to let old issues push you apart. Right from the get-go you must communicate honestly what you need from each other. This is essential to having a successful long-term relationship.

The main thing to remember with any relationship you want to repair during a Mars retrograde is to be patient. This is a key ingredient to getting back on the same page. Why? Because there is likely an underlying tension or even anger that might erupt at any time. So it is wise to move patiently to slow down your reaction time. Don't be timid in asking for the time you need to feel comfortable in reentering a partnership with a person. Business connections don't normally contain the same emotional intensity as more intimate encounters. But then again, sometimes they do. Think and take action to bring harmony into situations and you will be well on your way to creating relationships you will enjoy.

Mars Turning Direct:
The Jet Lag Following the Mars Retrograde

You more than likely will let out a big sigh of relief when Mars finally finishes up its two-month retrograde cycle. Your feet may seem to be more in step with your thoughts the way you are accustomed to. Your goals will feel like they have switched into a higher gear. It is okay to raise a glass in a celebration toast that another Mars retrograde has concluded.

There is likely going to be a tendency in the first days of Mars turned direct to look back at your actions of the past two months. You may require a week or so after the Mars retrograde time period to feel like you are in the here and now as far as getting new things initiated. There might be a feeling similar to jet lag as Mars is moving into its direct motion. Your body and mind are trying to reconfigure to get into sync with this direct motion. Don't be overly concerned if you feel a little more fatigued than usual as Mars first returns to being direct again. Everyone else is probably undergoing the same process. Even if their actions don't really show this, you can count on everyone trying to get back to their normal direct way of getting things done. So be patient with yourself and others. It does take a little time to adjust to the energy of Mars moving from retrograde back to direct motion.

If you need more rest than usual in the first few days of Mars moving direct, don't be surprised. People you are close to might be feeling a need to move slower. If you are ordinarily a fast-paced person, it won't take that long to be moving more briskly mentally and physically. If you happen to be a slower-paced type, it could take slightly longer to get moving with intensity. Don't worry. It does not take long for fiery Mars to motivate you to pick up any slack from a retrograde. It will snap you out of any hesitation to put your best foot forward. Mars has a capacity to inspire you to go from zero to sixty in a matter of seconds.

Try not to obsess over what you did not get done while Mars was retrograde. You can make up for any lost time very quickly. The direct motion of Mars can activate your get-up-and-go better than any other planet. Mars can actually push you to move faster than you would prefer one week into its direct motion! It is as though the two-month Mars retrograde was one big gigantic inhale and now you are ready to blow out an expansive exhale. This does not mean that you did nothing worthwhile while Mars was traveling retrograde, but only that the energy expression is now different, meaning you are ready to act with greater spontaneity. Your impulse to take a risk intensifies.

You won't exhibit the same thinking and behavior during every Mars retrograde. Each of these cycles is unique. There will be certain instances when you will be ready to act quickly on an idea even while Mars is retrograde. This is a real possibility. Your mind, body, and spirit are immediately ready to take off for new horizons. However, there will also be those Mars retrogrades that find you putting your plans on hold. Your instincts will sense it is better to wait for a more opportune time to act on an idea. These are the Mars retrogrades that probably led you to examine deeply your inner motivations for actions. But there is no need to be overly worried. When Mars does turn direct, you can take what you learned while Mars was retrograde and pour it passionately into the direct motion of this planet. So you see it all can still work out in the end in a positive way for you.

Correcting Missteps During a Mars Retrograde

When you realize you made a mistake during a Mars retrograde, what should you do? This may have occurred when you were right in the middle of a Mars retrograde and wish you had not taken a wrong turn for what appears now to have been for the worst. For one thing, try not to get too overwhelmed by this. You can retrace your steps. If you got in too big of a hurry during this retrograde time period, that is not so unusual. It is easy to miss key details no matter how careful you thought you performed an action. You will waste time and energy if you beat yourself up too much for a misstep. Try not to blame others for a dilemma that presents itself. That will only further compound the problem. Staying centered and calm is the best approach to going back and walking in the right direction again. You need to take a deep breath or call a timeout. If you rush too fast with a solution, you may make matters worse.

Perhaps you were not assertive enough and this caused you to make a bad choice. Try to remember that Mars is the planet capable of assisting you to ask for what you really need. You don't need to settle for a lot less than required to be successful in getting what you need. Life in many respects is a series of negotiations. You won't always get your own way. Compromise is often needed to make you and someone else feel like you got a fair deal. But not being assertive during a Mars retrograde leads to trouble. You must exercise a solid degree of decisiveness to make winning choices.

A lack of patience is often the cause of getting out of step with a Mars retrograde. Anxiousness about the outcome of a plan will cause you not to see the entire picture clearly. To bring it into better focus, you sometimes need to slow down during a Mars retrograde. Your impulses can be too far out in front of the reality you seek. Getting things done without having to do a repeat performance is often accomplished by taking a slower pace. There is an old saying to "move quickly but don't rush". This is an excellent mantra to successfully navigate a Mars retrograde.

Positive and Negative Ways to Experience a Mars Retrograde	
Positive Expression	*Negative Expression*
Appropriate release of anger	Explosive release of anger
Assertiveness	Too aggressive
Initiating plans	Lack of effort
Facing conflict	Running away from problems
Personal power	Loss of self in others
Learning patience	Extreme impatience

During the two months of a Mars retrograde, it may seem at times like you are taking one step forward and two steps backward in your everyday life. With patience and a little persistence you can steer around much of the frustration that you could experience during this Mars retrograde cycle.

Anger is a key Mars theme. During a Mars retrograde, anger can build more than you realize over situations that you don't like. You want to be sure not to let this raw emotion get the best of you. If you sit with anger for too long, it is not good for your mental and physical well-being. It has a way of coming out at the wrong people and at the wrong time if you lose touch with how you are feeling. One of the best remedies is to communicate clearly with others what is bothering you. This may seem difficult during a Mars retrograde. Holding back your true feelings can later become explosive anger, so do the best you can in being direct in the moment.

During a Mars retrograde, being assertive without being too aggressive is a good goal. If you are too timid, people won't know how to fulfill your needs. If you are too demanding and crave too much attention, others will resist your requests. Finding the middle ground between being too pushy and not being assertive enough is the answer to this possible dilemma. If you hide your talents, you will miss opportunities during a Mars retrograde. A show of arrogance will turn others off. The main message here is to promote your ability without tooting your horn so loudly that it grows annoying.

Getting a plan out of the starting gate takes extra effort during a Mars retrograde. Your intensity to initiate the right amount of energy to put a plan into action may be lacking. Don't panic. This is likely happening to many other people as well during this retrograde cycle. You may need some rest before you start again. Or you might need to overcome a fear of failure and throw caution to the wind. The bottom line is that you need to find the inspiration to put your goals into motion.

Problems sometimes seem harder to confront during a Mars retrograde. You might want them to magically disappear. You don't want to let a fear of conflict rule you. Many times it is the hesitation that makes a difficult situation larger than it is in reality. Facing adversity often will make you internally stronger. So you see there is a payoff for dealing with issues as they appear. You could be surprised during a Mars retrograde when in confronting a crisis you realize it was not that big of a problem.

Personal power is another Mars theme. It's not that you are likely to completely lose touch with your own needs during a Mars retrograde, but there is a chance you may look for too much empowerment from other people. Your sense of independence can get lost if you are constantly looking for someone else to make you stronger. When you realize you are a complete person with unique gifts, it frees you. Your creative power grows in intensity when you clarify your own identity.

Patience is testy during a Mars retrograde. This can be impatience with yourself or others. Be sure you are not over-reacting to what is occurring. This is not so unusual during a Mars retrograde. Your reaction time to the words and actions of others might be a lot faster than usual. There will be Mars retrogrades where you find yourself being too patient. Cutting people a lot of slack can backfire, especially if it turns out they don't have your best interests in mind. With a lot of practice you can become an expert at knowing when to be patient and when to say enough is enough.

Mars Stationary Motion

When Mars appears to be standing still when viewed from the earth, it is referred to as having stationary movement. This motionless appearance occurs when the Mars orbit is either about to reverse its movement from direct to retrograde (called stationary retrograde) or from retrograde to direct (called stationary direct). In reality, Mars does not change direction or stop moving. It just shows us this illusion in the sky. The standing still is known as a planet's station. A Mars station, when it remains motionless, lasts for three days when it is about to change direction either from retrograde to direct or direct to retrograde.

When Mars is bracing to move from direct to retrograde motion and is in a stationary position for three days, it is natural not to be as quick to take action on an idea. As a matter of fact, it is usually wise to think with extra forethought before leaping. Patience will save you much time and energy and will prevent you from getting angry at yourself and others. Don't let your emotions rule you during these few days. Rather than rush, use this brief amount of time to consider all of your options. If you slow down, your sense of timing will be sharper. Your mind and intuition will find it easier to guide you to success. You don't have to stop all of your activities. Remember to stay focused and keep your expectations realistic.

When Mars is pushing with great force to move from retrograde to direct motion and remaining painstakingly stationary direct for three days, you may sense this same push to move forward with a plan. Your reluctance to take a risk can seem like it has disappeared. It might feel like whatever was holding you back is no longer in your way. A renewed feistiness to show the world your ability can manifest. Decisiveness is more readily available. But do exercise patience. People may seem to move too slowly. Don't grow too aggressive. It is okay to show self-confidence. Include those you love in your decisions and they are more likely to be supportive. But then again, you are not going to be in the mood to ask others for permission to embrace your own creative power.

The Silver Lining Following a Mars Retrograde

What benefits can you derive from surviving the challenge presented by a Mars retrograde? These two months provide an opportunity to *recharge your inspiration to pursue your goals*. A more tempered vigor to put a plan into action does not imply you will miss a step when Mars turns direct following this retrograde cycle. Think of this as the universe's way of offering you the impetus to be wiser about taking action. In other words, before you take a leap forward, perhaps you will gain insight into whether something is really worth your time and energy.

Not long after a Mars retrograde finishes having its way with you, it is very likely that you will feel a sense of renewal. The inward empowering potential of a Mars retrograde is not so obvious when you are in the backward cycle. You may slowly become more conscious of how the Mars retrograde revealed the steps to take to let go of anger issues so you can proceed ahead with greater clarity. As you once again experience the Mars direct movement, your anxiety about taking action to put your goals into forward motion can find greater confidence.

Don't ever underestimate the potential of Mars retrograde to heal old inner wounds. Emotional pain can be lessened. Your assertiveness can be bolstered and your patience strengthened. Your identity can find a new illumination. A Mars retrograde fills you with the resolve to believe in your capabilities to attract a more abundant life, which is a wonderful silver lining.

Chapter Five

Quick Answers to Your Retrograde Questions

This chapter will provide you with answers to the most commonly asked questions about retrograde planets. You can refer to this section as often as needed to help you make important decisions in planning your life during a retrograde cycle. When you want to move forward with a plan, timing will be aided by this convenient reference guide. You can always act on a goal during a retrograde. The thing to remember is try to work out as many of the details before the retrograde begins.

Should I Sign a Contract During a Retrograde?

During a Mercury retrograde, be extra careful with written agreements. If you must sign a contract or written commitment, then be sure to read all of the fine print. Hidden details could come back to bite you later. There will be those times in your life when you will have to sign a contract during a Mercury retrograde. Take your time and be sure you truly understand everything required of you. If you are signing a type of short-term deal, it might not be as big of a problem. But if you are entering into a long-term arrangement, then this is when you must be very certain you are clear about what you are getting into. The bottom line is that during a Mercury retrograde you can sign a contract, but wear your most focused business hat to make sure you see the entire picture.

Should I Get Married During a Retrograde?

If you have to get married during a Mercury retrograde, just make sure all of the invitations have been mailed out before Mercury turns retrograde. The event can go well if you don't wait until Mercury retrograde to do most of the planning. There are times in life when you have to move forward with an important milestone during a retrograde cycle. The key thing to remember here is taking care of the most vital details before the retrograde starts. Don't be surprised if something does need to be changed after the retrograde begins. Don't panic. Stay centered and calm and everything will likely work out just fine. Your perfectionist tendencies will be highlighted, so you could think things are not going as well as expected. Chances are if you planned well the event is going much better than it might appear. Focus on the joy and happiness you seek and don't worry if something does not go as planned. Think positive and you will be pleased with the final results.

What if you are getting married during a Venus retrograde? Venus is associated with partnerships and especially marriage. Make the crucial decisions before the retrograde begins if at all possible. You don't want to get bogged down with the indecision that a Venus retrograde could present to you.

The type of atmosphere you are trying to create for the event needs to be well thought out before Venus turns retrograde to ensure you will be happy with the outcome. The wedding cake, attire, and food are other key Venus arenas. Work out all of the details before the retrograde as much as possible. Make sure you only invite people who truly are coming to celebrate your union with your partner. If you are traveling to go on a honeymoon, make sure this is arranged before the Venus retrograde starts.

Should I Accept a New Job During a Retrograde?

If you are offered a new job during a Mercury retrograde and it is a great opportunity, then absolutely accept it. Just be sure you are clear about what the job really entails. Are there any hidden factors you may not know about? If it is a path to a better future, then go for it. It could be that you need a better work environment and more stimulating work. The Mercury retrograde might be opening a new door for this to occur.

Venus is connected to work as much as to relationships. A Venus retrograde might be paving the road to a more abundant life. Increasing your earning power is a motivating force to get you to accept a new job. A Venus retrograde does present a challenge in getting you to leave a comfort zone. You may need an extra push from others to get you to take advantage of a new work opportunity. Perhaps it means just as much to you to have a better team of people to work with on a daily basis. A Venus retrograde may point you to a job that offers this. If you are given a chance to move into a new place of employment that will help you to better afford what you need to buy and to pay all of your bills, then don't let a Venus retrograde stop you from creating a better life.

Can I Have Surgery During a Retrograde?

Yes, you can have a surgery during a Mercury retrograde. If you have the luxury of planning when you want to have an elective surgery, try to pick a date when you won't feel too conflicted about your schedule. If it is a surgery that does not require a long recovery time, it probably won't matter if you have a procedure done during a Mercury retrograde. If you are going to need a longer time to rest after a more major operation, then the best advice would be to clear as much of your schedule as possible. You want to make sure you don't get worried about your work or other responsibilities. If you are going to require a place to fully rehabilitate, pick a place that best suits your needs if at all possible. If you are going to go home after a surgery to recover, make sure you have everything set up to keep you as comforted as possible. Planning in advance is always wise before Mercury turns retrograde.

Having a surgery performed during a Mars retrograde has certain advantages. It can actually make a recovery go better. Your body can find it easier to accept the healing process during a Mars retrograde. It is as though it knows how to automatically get into repair mode. Be sure you accept a slowdown in daily living even if you are normally a restless soul always wanting to be on the go. If some exercise is required, you can find this to be not that difficult a challenge under the gaze of a Mars retrograde. Try to follow the prescribed amount of physical activity rather than push yourself way overboard.

This particular retrograde cycle might be when you finally decide it is time to move ahead with a surgery you had been putting off.

Can I Begin a New Relationship During a Retrograde?

If you start a new relationship during a Mercury retrograde, make your best effort to communicate clearly. Your curiosity about someone can intensify. It is okay to keep the communication on the lighter side. A getting-to-know-you beginning can be a fun experience for you and a partner. Sharing your favorite topics of interest is stimulating during this retrograde cycle. Sometimes people do meet in interesting and surprising ways during a Mercury retrograde. Don't hold back in discussing a wide range of subjects.

Likewise, it is okay to begin a new relationship during a Venus retrograde. You may feel like you have known the person before even though you just met. If you have shared values and a tolerance for your differences, you probably will sense this fast. If this is a passionate attraction that gets the relationship off to a fast start, don't be surprised if you feel a need to slow things down a bit. This often does occur during a Venus retrograde. Creating a romantic atmosphere during a Venus retrograde brings you closer quickly. Don't force a relationship to go too fast, but then again, you don't need to fear being assertive. If you focus more on making a new friend, it works well in connecting over mutual life interests. A Venus retrograde can stimulate a desire for companionship.

Can I Buy a New Car During a Retrograde?

Mercury is a transportation and travel planet. Therefore, buying a new car during a Mercury retrograde means you need to be extra clear about what you need. Wearing your negotiating hat and focusing on getting a good deal is wise. It is a good idea to already have your mind made up about the particular car you want to buy. If you have any doubt at all, it is better to wait until this planet turns direct. Patience is something to keep very much in mind. Contracts come under the rulership of Mercury as well, which is another great reason to take your time and go slowly if you are trying to buy a car during a Mercury retrograde. Don't allow a salesperson to pressure you into a purchase you are not sure about. You can buy a car during a Mercury retrograde if the right deal presents itself for a car you already knew you wanted.

If Venus happens to be retrograde, having your loan already prearranged with a lender before you buy a car is smart. This could keep you within your budget and prevent you from getting a high interest rate if you are going to make payments on a car. Venus is associated with our sense of color and our taste in what we like to own. If you already know the style and color of the car you want to buy, it will keep you from being too indecisive during a Venus retrograde. Remember you are trying to negotiate the best deal for yourself.

Can I Buy a New Computer During a Retrograde?

Mercury is a powerhouse of a communication planet. During its retrograde cycle, you can successfully buy a new computer. Be sure it is exactly what you need in terms of processing speed and memory size and any useful software packages included that you find essential to utilize. Pay extra attention to the return policy just in case you aren't happy with the way the computer is operating. Do your research thoroughly before Mercury turns retrograde to avoid making the wrong purchase. It would be great if technical support was included free of charge.

Can I Close on My House During a Retrograde?

It isn't so unusual to sign the final papers to close the deal on buying a house during a Mercury retrograde. There are often delays for one reason or another in purchasing a house that can push you into a Mercury retrograde time period. If you have had a good inspection done and asked for any repairs to be finished, then you can certainly complete the buying of a house during a Mercury retrograde. Even if you are buying a new house, be sure everything is pretty much the way you like it.

Can I Go on Vacation During a Retrograde?

If you are planning to go on vacation during a Mercury retrograde, try to work out all of the details ahead of time. Do your research about where you are staying before Mercury turns retrograde. If you are returning to a place you have already visited in the past, it is more likely that everything will go smoothly. If this is a new experience, then just be extra careful with your planning.

Can I Submit a College Application During a Retrograde?

During a Mercury retrograde you want to be sure you answer all questions very thoughtfully and thoroughly even more so than usual. Don't be surprised if you are changing your answers from one day to the next. The best advice is to go slowly and patiently. Mercury is a planet that encourages all of us to consider more than one option. A Mercury retrograde may stimulate you to apply to more than one college. This is especially true if you are applying to a school that is difficult to get into. Stay confident. Don't doubt yourself. If completing an essay about a subject of interest is part of your application process, it is wise during a Mercury retrograde to get someone to read it. Having another set of eyes look at your writing may provide you with important input to make your essay even better. Be sure to emphasize your talents and any awards. It is not unusual during a Mercury retrograde to remember more of your special skills and abilities.

Can I Submit a Book or Business Proposal During a Retrograde?

A Mercury retrograde can actually give you an extra edge in refining a book or business proposal of any type. How you want to present yourself and your subject matter might need a tweak, so Mercury retrograde is a good time to edit a document or business idea before presenting it. If you have gone over a written proposal thoroughly, you can submit it during a Mercury retrograde. This communication giant of a planet can still come through for you during its retrograde cycle. One final comment is that if you can possibly delay until this planet turns direct before doing a presentation, it would be wise to wait. Why? Because you might see an even better way to improve your written pages and concepts during the retrograde.

Should I Be Careful before Sending Messages on Social Media?

The answer is absolutely! It does not mean you have to stay off social media during a retrograde cycle. But then again, you don't want to regret something you posted on Facebook, emailed, texted, or tweeted when angry or feeling very emotional during a Mercury, Venus, or Mars retrograde. You will likely have at least one day during one of these retrograde time periods when you are not on top of your game. It happens.

During the three weeks of a Mercury retrograde, be sure you are clear about what you are sending. Does your message clearly state your opinions or ideas? Make sure you really are accurately perceiving what someone else is sending you before responding. It takes extra effort during a Mercury retrograde to communicate clearly with others. If you take your time, even if it means reflecting one extra minute before responding, your words will likely be sent with your true intention and will be better received by others.

When contacting friends, lovers, family members, or business colleagues during the six weeks of a Venus retrograde, it is a good idea to be mentally centered if you are going to discuss a sensitive issue. Focus on achieving harmony and you will be more likely to send messages that produce good results. Send words that serve to bring win-win results for you and someone else. Venus is the great mediator of the sky. Seek unity and you will be able to win admiration rather than cause unnecessary friction. You can still arrange social events with others during a Venus retrograde. Your romantic imagination can be just as awesome as usual.

During the two months of a Mars retrograde, control your impulses before hitting the send button! There can be a tendency to be in a big rush to make a point. Just be sure you are not sending messages that are angry reactions that lack clear thinking. You could cause more trouble than it is worth. With some patience, you can use a Mars retrograde time period to get what you need from others. Business negotiations can be performed successfully at this time. Mars brings out our passionate responses, so exercise some caution when sending messages during a Mars retrograde if you are upset about a situation.

Conclusion

My main purpose in writing this book was to help you navigate your way through retrograde time periods with less anxiety. Another key reason was to help guide you in the form of survival tips so you can get the most from your creative energy. You can refer back to the survival tips for a retrograde cycle whenever needed. The retrograde movement of a planet need not interfere with your goals. The retrograde cycle of a planet teaches each of us to exercise patience in making decisions. Making the most of a retrograde time period comes with practice. Remember not to panic. There is nothing inherently negative about a planet's retrograde movement. On the contrary, you might discover some of your greatest insights during these retrograde visits.

Don't forget to use the many survival tips described in this book. No retrograde time period will operate exactly like a previous one. Each is unique. If you do run into a challenge during one of the Mercury, Venus, or Mars retrograde planetary movements, refer to this book as much as needed. It was written as a handy reference to be used by you over and over again whenever you need it. I wish you the best of luck in pursuing all of your hopes and dreams!

To Write the Author

If you wish to contact the author or would like more information about this book, please write to the author in care of Llewellyn Worldwide Ltd., and we will forward your request. Both the author and publisher appreciate hearing from you and learning of your enjoyment of this book and how it has helped you. Llewellyn Worldwide Ltd. cannot guarantee that every letter written to the author can be answered, but all will be forwarded. Please write to:

Bernie Ashman
% Llewellyn Worldwide
2143 Wooddale Drive
Woodbury, MN 55125-2989

Please enclose a self-addressed stamped envelope for reply,
or $1.00 to cover costs. If outside the U.S.A., enclose
an international postal reply coupon.

GET MORE AT **LLEWELLYN.COM**

Visit us online to browse hundreds of our books and decks, plus sign up to receive our e-newsletters and exclusive online offers.

- Free tarot readings • Spell-a-Day • Moon phases
- Recipes, spells, and tips • Blogs • Encyclopedia
- Author interviews, articles, and upcoming events

GET SOCIAL WITH **LLEWELLYN**

 Find us on Facebook

www.Facebook.com/LlewellynBooks

Follow us on

www.Twitter.com/Llewellynbooks

GET BOOKS AT **LLEWELLYN**

LLEWELLYN ORDERING INFORMATION

Order online: Visit our website at www.llewellyn.com to select your books and place an order on our secure server.

Order by phone:
- Call toll free within the U.S. at 1-877-NEW-WRLD (1-877-639-9753)
- Call toll free within Canada at 1-866-NEW-WRLD (1-866-639-9753)
- We accept VISA, MasterCard, and American Express

Order by mail:
Send the full price of your order (MN residents add 6.875% sales tax) in U.S. funds, plus postage and handling to: Llewellyn Worldwide, 2143 Wooddale Drive Woodbury, MN 55125-2989

POSTAGE AND HANDLING

STANDARD (U.S. & Canada):
(Please allow 12 business days)
$25.00 and under, add $4.00.
$25.01 and over, FREE SHIPPING.

INTERNATIONAL ORDERS (airmail only):
$16.00 for one book, plus $3.00 for each additional book.

Visit us online for more shipping options. Prices subject to change.

FREE CATALOG!

To order, call
1-877-
NEW-WRLD
ext. 8236
or visit our
website

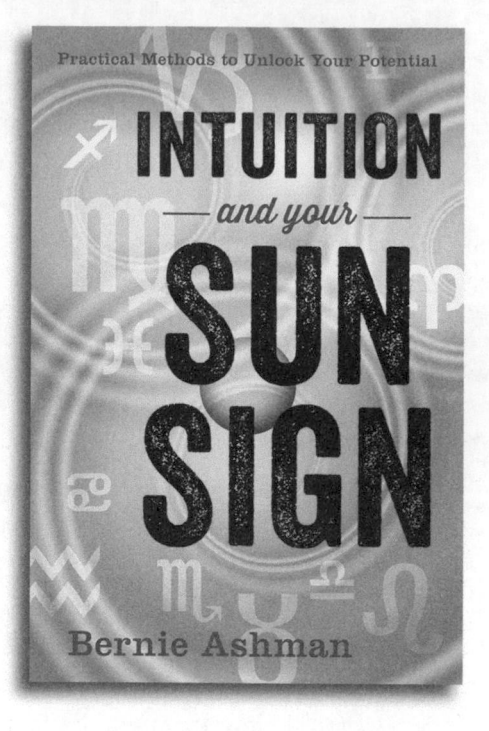

Practical Methods to Unlock Your Potential

INTUITION
—and your—
SUN SIGN

Bernie Ashman

Intuition and Your Sun Sign
Practical Methods to Unlock Your Potential
BERNIE ASHMAN

Your hidden spiritual and practical gifts come alive when you make the most of your intuitive potential. Astrologer Bernie Ashman reveals how to use a basic understanding of astrology to instantly tap into and use your varied intuitive gifts to overcome blocks and find the mental clarity you seek.

You'll need no astrological background to make use of this information in practical situations. Even more excitingly, you'll develop your own insights and intuition about others, letting you make better choices quickly and more easily, raising your self-confidence. Looking at someone else's sun sign will allow you to communicate with them better, bringing improved harmony and understanding to your relationships. You'll master challenges, improve your imagination, achieve goals, and find personal empowerment.

978-0-7387-3894-9, 360 pp., 6 x 9 $18.99

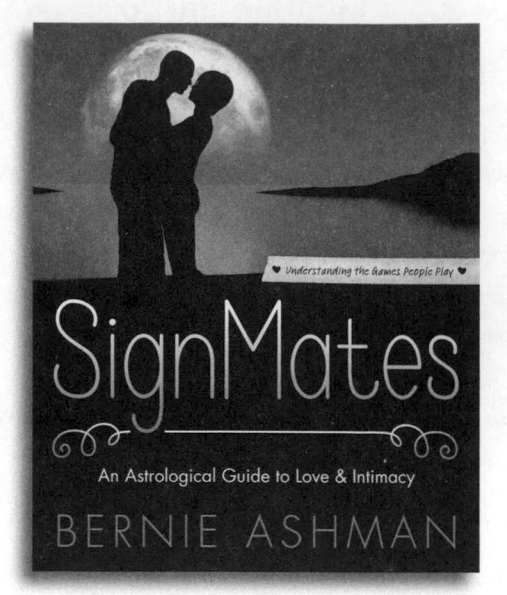

♥ Understanding the Games People Play ♥

SignMates

An Astrological Guide to Love & Intimacy

BERNIE ASHMAN

SignMates
An Astrological Guide to Love & Intimacy
BERNIE ASHMAN

Stepping far beyond the typical lists of "Leo gets along with…
but is incompatible with…", *SignMates* points out the hurtful
"games" that any two signs are likely to play, gives strategies for
overcoming them, and points the way to the "rainbow"—the
happy ending of being real with each other every day.

978-1-56718-046-6, 504 pp., 7½ x 9⅛   **$21.99**

LLEWELLYN'S

COMPLETE BOOK OF
ASTROLOGY

THE EASY WAY TO LEARN ASTROLOGY

KRIS BRANDT RISKE, M.A.

Lewellyn's Complete Book of Astrology
The Easy Way to Learn Astrology
KRIS BRANDT RISKE, MA

The horoscope is filled with insights into personal traits, talents, and life possibilities. With *Llewellyn's Complete Book of Astrology*, you can learn to read and understand this amazing cosmic road map for yourself and others.

Professional astrologer Kris Brandt Riske introduces the many mysterious parts that make up the horoscope, devoting special attention to three popular areas of interest: relationships, career, and money. Friendly and easy to follow, this comprehensive book guides you to explore the zodiac signs, planets, houses, and aspects, and teaches how to synthesize this valuable information. Riske also explores the history of astrology going back to the ancient Babylonians, in addition to the different branches of contemporary astrology.

Once you learn the language of astrology, you'll be able to read birth charts of yourself and others, determine compatibility between two people, track your earning potential, uncover areas of opportunity or challenge, and analyze your career path.

978-0-7387-1071-6, 336 pp., 8 x 10   **$19.99**

LLEWELLYN'S

COMPLETE BOOK OF PREDICTIVE

ASTROLOGY

THE EASY WAY TO PREDICT YOUR FUTURE

☆ KRIS BRANDT RISKE, M.A. ☆

Llewellyn's Complete Book
of Predictive Astrology
The Easy Way to Predict Your Future
KRIS BRANDT RISKE, MA

Find out what potential the future holds and use those insights to create the life you desire with this definitive guide to predictive astrology.

In her signature easy-to-understand style, popular astrologer Kris Brandt Riske offers step-by-step instructions for performing each major predictive technique—solar arcs, progressions, transits, lunar cycles, and planetary returns—along with an introduction to horary astrology. Discover how to read all elements of a predictive chart and pinpoint when changes in your career, relationships, finances, and other important areas of life are on the horizon.

Also includes several example charts based on the lives of the author's clients and celebrities such as Marilyn Monroe, Martha Stewart, and Pamela Anderson.

978-0-7387-2755-4, 288 pp., 8 x 10   **$18.95**

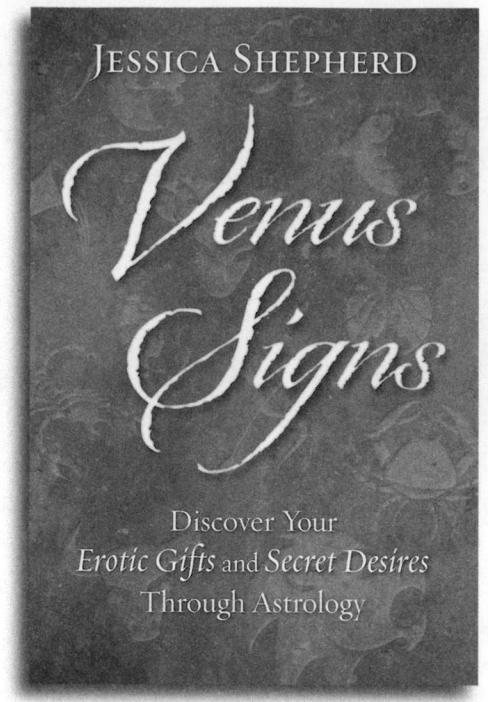

JESSICA SHEPHERD

Venus Signs

Discover Your
Erotic Gifts and *Secret Desires*
Through Astrology

Venus Signs
Discover Your Erotic Gifts and Secret Desires Through Astrology
JESSICA SHEPHERD

Take an intimate tour of the inner world of all twelve Venus signs. For millennia, Venus swaggered through the history books with unrivaled self-possession and sexual self-confidence, as notorious for seducing others as making her own pleasure and enjoyment central. Yet many women today have lost touch with the very aspects of our self she represents: joy, self-worth, sexual vitality, and eroticism.

In *Venus Signs*, Jessica breathes life back into the Goddess. As she leads you through a personal journey into the Venus sign of your self and your loved ones, prepare to become reacquainted with your innermost secret desires and your erotic strengths. Discover the must-have qualities of your soul mates, how to keep a long-term relationship happily humming, how to align with your own feminine energy, and how to draw your deepest heart's desires toward you. These are Venus powers that you can use to create, laugh, and love exceptionally well!

978-0-7387-4194-9, 240 pp., 6 x 9 **$16.99**

sun signs
& soul mates

An Astrological Guide to Relationships

LINDA GEORGE

Sun Signs & Soul Mates
An Astrological Guide to Relationships
LINDA GEORGE

Today's overly materialistic and ego-centered world makes it difficult to recognize our inner selves, let alone connect on a spiritual level with another person. Thankfully, astrology reveals the true patterns in ourselves and in others.

Evolutionary astrologer Linda George looks at the nature of the soul and relationships through the lens of astrology, exploring the lighter and darker sides of the twelve Sun signs of the zodiac. She reveals the compatibility potential for each pairing and offers entertaining and insightful relationship clues to help you better relate to your partner. Learn about each Sun sign's strengths, challenges, and behavioral quirks. From deciding whether to date that flirtatious Gemini to identifying your soul's fundamental needs, *Sun Signs & Soul Mates* will help you understand yourself—and your partner—more completely.

978-0-7387-1558-2, 240 pp., 6 x 9   **$17.95**

To order, call 1-877-NEW-WRLD
Prices subject to change without notice
Order at Llewellyn.com 24 hours a day, 7 days a week!

JOANN HAMPAR

astrology
for beginners

A SIMPLE WAY TO READ YOUR CHART

Astrology for Beginners
A Simple Way to Read Your Chart
JOANN HAMPAR

Getting a glimpse of your own astrological chart isn't a challenge these days. The tough part is finding meaning in this complex diagram of symbols.

In *Astrology for Beginners,* Joann Hampar shows that interpreting your birth chart is actually easy. Emphasizing a practical approach, this step-by-step guide takes you effortlessly through the language of astrological symbols. As each chapter unfolds, a new realm of your horoscope will be revealed, including chart patterns, zodiac signs, houses, planets, and aspects. By the last lesson, you'll be able to read and interpret your chart—what originally looked like a jumble of symbols—and gain valuable insight into yourself and others.

978-0-7387-1106-5, 240 pp., 6 x 9   **$14.95**

Astrology
Understanding the Birth Chart
KEVIN BURK

In *Astrology: Understanding the Birth Chart*, Kevin Burk takes you step-by-step from the core basics to the finer complexities of chart interpretation while avoiding sidetracks into obscure techniques and fuzzy thinking. As a teacher, Burk also understands that a real grasp of the subject entails more than just learning the techniques-it also involves grasping the underlying principles that make those techniques valid.

978-1-56718-088-6, 386 pp., 7½ x 9⅛   **$21.99**

Astrology of the Moon
An Illuminating Journey Through the Signs and Houses
AMY HERRING

Your Moon sign represents your emotional nature and lights the way toward profound spiritual growth. With *Astrology of the Moon*, you can identify your core emotional needs, learn to fulfill them, and make the best choices for a more rewarding, spiritually enriched life.

Focusing on the natal and progressed Moon relationship, this information-packed guide explains the Moon's powerful energetic potential in relation to the signs, houses, planets, and aspects. In an easy-to-use "cookbook" format, Herring lays out your emotional needs in the areas of love, family life, your career, and more, with practical ways to meet these essential needs so you can create happiness at every stage of life.

978-0-7387-1896-5, 312 pp., 6 x 9   **$21.95**
